The Dutch Courtesan

THE NEW MERMAIDS

General Editor: Brian Gibbons
Professor of English Literature, University of Münster

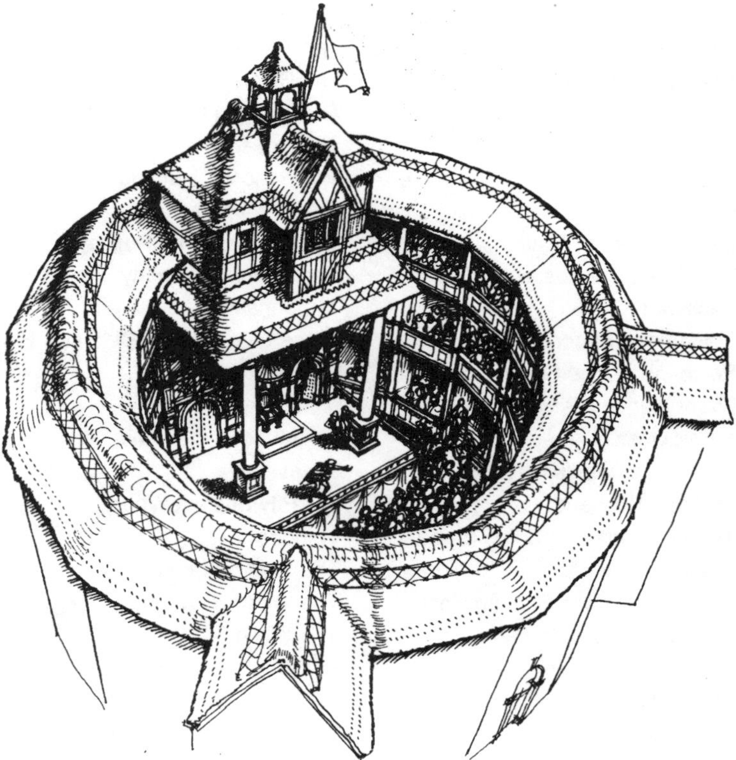

Reconstruction of an Elizabethan theatre by C. Walter Hodges

THE NEW MERMAIDS

The Alchemist
All for Love
Arden of Faversham
The Atheist's Tragedy
Bartholmew Fair
The Beaux' Stratagem
The Broken Heart
Bussy D'Ambois
The Changeling
A Chaste Maid in Cheapside
The Country Wife
The Critic
The Devil's Law-Case
The Double-Dealer
Dr Faustus
The Duchess of Malfi
The Dutch Courtesan
Eastward Ho!
Edward the Second
Epicoene *or* The Silent Woman
Every Man in His Humour
A Fair Quarrel
Gammer Gurton's Needle
An Ideal Husband
The Importance of Being Earnest
The Jew of Malta
The Knight of the Burning Pestle
Lady Windermere's Fan
London Assurance
Love for Love
The Malcontent
The Man of Mode
Marriage A-la-Mode
A New Way to Pay Old Debts
The Old Wife's Tale
The Plain Dealer
The Playboy of the Western World
The Provoked Wife
The Recruiting Officer
The Relapse
The Revenger's Tragedy
The Rivals
The Roaring Girl
The Rover
The School for Scandal
She Stoops to Conquer
The Shoemaker's Holiday
The Spanish Tragedy
Tamburlaine
Three Late Medieval Morality Plays
  Mankind
  Everyman
  Mundus et Infans
Thyestes
'Tis Pity She's a Whore
Volpone
The Way of the World
The White Devil
The Witch
A Woman Killed with Kindness
A Woman of No Importance
Women Beware Women

The Dutch Courtesan

JOHN MARSTON

Edited by

DAVID CRANE

Research Fellow in the University of Wales at Lampeter

LONDON / A & C BLACK

NEW YORK / W W NORTON

First New Mermaid edition published 1997
A & C Black (Publishers) Limited
35 Bedford Row, London WC1R 4JH
ISBN 0-7136-4475-3

Published in the United States of America by
W. W. Norton and Company Inc.
500 Fifth Avenue, New York, NY 10110
ISBN 0-393-90086-X

CIP catalogue records for this book
are available from the British Library
and the Library of Congress.

Typeset in 10pt Plantin by Fakenham Photosetting Ltd,
Fakenham, Norfolk
Printed & bound in Great Britain by
Creative Print and Design Wales
(Book Division), Ebbw Vale

CONTENTS

ACKNOWLEDGEMENTS

I am greatly indebted to previous editors of this play, and have in particular consulted the editions by Martin Wine and by Jackson and Neill. I have also been immensely helped by Professor Tom Craik's many acute suggestions on textual and commentary matters.

ABBREVIATIONS

Bullen	*The Works of John Marston*, ed. A. H. Bullen (3 vols., London, 1887)
Chambers	E. K. Chambers, *The Elizabethan Stage* (4 vols., London, 1923)
Davison	John Marston, *The Dutch Courtesan*, ed. Peter Davison (Edinburgh, 1968)
Hughes and Scouten	Leo Hughes and Arthur H. Scouten, 'Some Theatrical Adaptations of a Picaresque Tale', *Studies in English* 26 (Austin, Texas, 1945–6), pp. 98–114
Jackson and Neill	*The Selected Plays of John Marston*, ed. Macdonald P. Jackson and Michael Neill (Cambridge University Press, 1986)
Montaigne	*The Essayes of Michael Lord of Montaigne done into English by John Florio*, ed. Thomas Seccombe (3 vols., London, 1908) (references are by volume, chapter and page to this edition; the volume and chapter part of the reference also designates Montaigne's own division of his work)
OED	*Oxford English Dictionary*
Scott	Michael Scott, *John Marston's Plays: Theme, Structure and Performance* (London, 1978)
Tilley	M. P. Tilley, *A Dictionary of Proverbs in England in the Sixteenth and Seventeenth Centuries* (University of Michigan Press, 1950)
Walley	*Early Seventeenth Century Plays, 1600–1642*, ed. H. R. Walley and J. H. Wilson (New York, 1930)
Wine	John Marston, *The Dutch Courtesan*, ed. Martin Wine, Regents Renaissance Drama Series (London, 1965)
Wood	*The Plays of John Marston*, ed. H. H. Wood (3 vols., Edinburgh, 1934–9)

INTRODUCTION

THE AUTHOR

John Marston was born in 1576 and baptised at Wardington in Oxfordshire on 7 October of that year. His father, after whom he was named, was from a family of Shropshire gentry and his mother, Mary Guarsi, the daughter of an Italian physician resident in England. His command of Italian came from his mother, who perhaps also spoke English with a foreign accent like Franceschina, and who may even have been passionately and violently expressive in the way that Franceschina is, a way we surely associate more with Italian than Dutch origin.

On 4 February 1592 Marston matriculated at Brasenose College, Oxford, and after taking his degree two years later he went to join his highly successful lawyer father at the Inns of Court, the Middle Temple, where it was intended that he should follow him in a legal career. From 1597 until his father's death in 1599 he shared his father's chambers in the Middle Temple (a not unusual practice) but it is clear already from John Marston Senior's will that the son's interests were not in the law. In a draft of the will the father bequeaths his law books to the son, to:

> him that deserveth them not, that is my wilful disobedient son, who I think will sell them rather than use them, although I took pains and had delight therein; God bless him and give him true knowledge of himself, and to forgo his delight in plays and vain studies and fooleries.[1]

It is clear that by the time of his father's death, Marston's delight was not only in frequenting plays but in writing for the stage. He had already tried his hand at satirical verse, and some of his work was among the satires burnt by order of the Archbishop of Canterbury and the Bishop of London in 1599; but in the same year he received payment of two pounds from Henslowe for contributions to a play, and soon he was writing for the company of boy actors called the Children of Paul's, for whom between 1599 and 1601 he wrote *Jack Drum's Entertainment*, *Antonio and Mellida*, *Antonio's Revenge* and *What You Will*.

After the accession of King James, Marston began writing for the rival boys' company, the Children of the Queen's Revels, which

[1] Quoted by Jackson and Neill, p. x.

was reorganised and given a new patent as successor to Queen Elizabeth's Children of the Chapel Royal in 1604. For them in their theatre at Blackfriars Marston wrote his two best plays, *The Malcontent* (1603/4) and *The Dutch Courtesan* (1605). These were followed by *The Fawn* (1605/6) and *Sophonisba* (1606) for the same company. When Marston quitted the stage in 1608, probably because of anti-Scottish satire offensive to the King for which he was briefly imprisoned in Newgate in June of that year, a last play, *The Insatiate Countess*, was left unfinished (it was later completed by William Barkstead and published in 1613). This was altogether his third major brush with the authorities because after the burning of his satires in 1599 he had also been in trouble for his part in the collaboration with Jonson and Chapman on *Eastward Ho* with its anti-Scottish satire in 1604, that collaboration marking a point of closeness in Marston's usually wittily hostile relations with Jonson.

Perhaps in 1608 Marston thought finally enough was enough and a less dangerous mode of life was to be preferred, but already about three years beforehand he had married Mary Wilkes, the daughter of one of James I's chaplains, (as Freevill marries Beatrice) and presumably begun the process of settling into respectability which began in earnest with his taking of Anglican orders in 1609, with a curacy at his father-in-law's living of Barford St Martin in Wiltshire. In 1616 he obtained the living of Christchurch in Hampshire and there remained until he resigned it to come to London again in 1631. He died in London in 1634 and was buried beside his father in the Temple Church, his father no doubt at last content with a son who was so far out of love with his former 'vain studies and fooleries' as to wish to remove his name from a collection of his plays published in 1633.[2] He was a long way then, plainly, from the mercurial, emotional, witty, aggressive boy of the Inns of Court who thirty years before at a Christmas celebration, in a way that uncannily reminds us of Freevill and Franceschina, had danced with a Spanish girl (foreign like his mother) and liked and loathed her:

> John Marston, the last Christmas he danced with Alderman More's wife's daughter, a Spaniard born; fell into a strange commendation of her wit and beauty. When he had done, she thought to pay him home, and told him she thought he was a poet. ' 'Tis true', said he, 'for poets feign and lie, and so did I when I commended your beauty, for you are exceeding foul.'[3]

[2] See p. xxxi.

[3] *The Diary of John Manningham*, ed. John Bruce (Camden Society, 1868) p. 86 (entry for 21 Nov 1602; text modernised).

DATE AND SOURCES

The Dutch Courtesan was entered in the Stationers' Register on 26 June 1605 'as yt was latelie presented at the Blacke Fryers' and the title page of the 1605 quarto introduces the text 'as it was playd in the Blacke-Friars, by the Children *of her Maiesties Reuels*'. These formulations seem to refer to a production of the play not long before it was printed. An earlier limiting date for the writing of the play can be set by the publication in 1603 of John Florio's translation of Montaigne's *Essays*, since this translation is extensively drawn on, as the commentary notes make clear. The boys' company at the Blackfriars was reorganised under its new name and given its patent on 4 February 1604,[4] so that if the wording on the title-page is not simply in 1605 an up-to-date designation of the company but a description of it at the point when *The Dutch Courtesan* was first produced, this brings the date of composition further forward. A reference in the text to the presence of Scotsmen at court 'this two year' (see II.iii.30n) seems to bring the date further forward still, since James I arrived in London in May 1603. All in all, then, a date of composition for the play in early 1605 seems most likely.

The source for the main plot of the play is one of the interpolated stories in the first book of Nicolas de Montreux' romance, *Les Bergeries de Juliette* (1585).[5] In Montreux' story what is central is the friendship between two young men, a Venetian called Dellio and a Frenchman called the Sieur de la Selve. The Frenchman falls suddenly in love with the courtesan, Cinthye, whom Dellio renounces for his friend's sake, settling instead upon the virtuous Angelicque. Cinthye's eventually frustrated plan of revenge against Dellio is very much as presented in Marston's play. What Marston took from Montreux, then, was a narrative framework, but what he did with that is his own creation, the product of his own thought about human passion and how it is to be understood.

As an influence upon that thought and as an enabler, an offerer of possibilities, Marston clearly found Montaigne's *Essays* of such importance that they must count almost as a second source for the main action of the play. The essay chiefly drawn upon is the fifth one of the third book, 'Sur des vers de Virgile', in which Montaigne contemplates his own experience of love and sexual passion with uninhibited frankness and so open-mindedly inspects received notions as to what human beings should do with such passions as to allow his actual human experience an emphatic voice. What

[4] See p. xii.

[5] John J. O'Connor, 'The Chief Source of Marston's *Dutch Courtesan*', *Studies in Philology* 54 (1957), pp. 509–15.

Marston has from Montaigne is not so much the French writer's own opinions as the sense that ready-made, authoritatively inherited moral positions cannot simply be adopted wholesale by an individual without reference to his own experience of being alive.[6]

For the energetic but less thoughtful sub-plot of the play there is no single source, except the sixty-sixth novel of the first volume of William Painter's *The Palace of Pleasure* (1566), which lies behind Cocledemoy's trickery with the goblet in III.iii. Other analogues in Elizabethan literature of low life have been suggested for the comic shaving scenes, the cloak business and the constables, but for these elements of his play Marston was really drawing upon a theatrical tradition in fluid solution all about him.[7]

THE INTELLECTUAL AND SOCIAL CONTEXT OF THE PLAY

An understanding of the theatrical circumstances of *The Dutch Courtesan* is, as we shall see later, essential to any complete grasp of the play; but there can be no sensitive and accurate feel for its central dynamic without some understanding, too, of the intellectual and social context in which Marston was writing. In common with many other sons of the gentry in late Elizabethan and Jacobean times, he had come to the Inns of Court from one of the universities as a boy in his late teens. There he found, in the most educated society in the capital, in what was described as the third university in the kingdom, an atmosphere very different from that of the two established universities. Even though the boys and young men among whom he lived in London had come ostensibly to study law and to be the docile pupils of their elders in an organised hierarchy of respect which the very nature of law encouraged, it being founded not only socially but intellectually upon precedent and custom, upon 'authoritatively inherited positions', that was not the whole story. In fact, most by far of those who came either had never had any intention from the beginning of following a legal career or, like Marston himself, were seduced away from it, so that for them the whole apparatus of the Inns of Court was no more than the means by which they could be away from home, away from the more oppressive discipline of an Oxford or Cambridge college, and in London.

[6] For an account of Montaigne that gives a sense of the kind of influence he might have had on Marston, see Harold Bloom, *The Western Canon* (New York, 1994) chap. 6.

[7] James J. Jackson, 'Sources of the Subplot of Marston's *The Dutch Courtesan*', *Philological Quarterly* 31 (1952), pp. 223–4.

So an atmosphere flourished among the young men of the Inns of Court that was only in a dilute form legal, and that dilution of solemnity, of authority, was in a manner encouraged by another aspect of the law itself. For the law, then as now, encourages rhetoric, encourages acting, encourages the trying out of positions as the case is made for prosecution or defence; it works in this respect not from a sense of 'what is' but from a sense of 'what if' (see III.i.16n). And so the fledgling lawyer might be encouraged to make a speech in defence of this position, or to make a speech in defence of that position, with a great deal more freedom than would have been the case in the dusty academic exercises of the universities.

That is a kind of rhetoric we find in *The Dutch Courtesan*, but in the play, as no doubt in the real life Marston was leading, this is not only a game but a real experiment conducted by young men trying out intellectual and moral positions to see how they can fit with the passions within. It is not at all surprising that the respectable Inns of Court should have encouraged their own entertainments, plays and revels, and should have provided, especially for the more gentlemanly private theatres, the most educated and aware audience for plays in the capital, for the study of law as it is to be practised in the courts needs a feel for improvisation, for audience (or jury) response, for what formulation or expression of opinion will elicit a response in this or that precise situation. And *The Dutch Courtesan* is a play turning on moments that, as it were, have no before or after, moments when *this* is the energetic, the *invited*, thing to be said.

Comedy it may be (in the sense that it comes to a neatly tied-off ending rather than that the main action causes mirth), but Marston's play is also serious in the way that young men may be serious in experimenting with the moral and intellectual positions in terms of which they will lead their future lives. The rhetorical atmosphere of the Inns of Court must have fed and nourished an experimenting with position that was also encouraged by the variety of possibility offered by the London streets all around.

Perhaps it may be, says the seventeen-year-old boy hesitating outside the brothel he itches to enter, that not all whores are the diseased and disgusting creatures of standard moralising, of authoritative precedent; what if a whore were instead 'a pretty, nimble-eyed Dutch Tanakin' (I.i.147–8)? How would my argument run then?

There were brothels within very easy reach of the Inns of Court, across the river by boat from the Temple stairs to Southwark, and no doubt the boy had friends in the Inn who used them and friends who did not, no doubt had friends who made speeches for them and friends who made speeches against them, the speeches against urging continence both for high-flown reasons to do with honour or not being damned and for the more telling reasons of avoiding the pox (or, as we might say, AIDS). No doubt, too, among those who made the speeches against were some who nevertheless went to whores. And no doubt the reverse was true also, that among those who made the speeches for were some for whom that was the full extent of their boldness.

Especially in the rhetorical atmosphere that flourished in the Inns of Court, it seems likely that the kind of trying out of position we see early in *The Dutch Courtesan* with Freevill and Malheureux would have been common, exciting, energetic. Of course, among the seniors in the Inn, the older men, the phenomenon would have been different; they would have grown into their positions, so that their views fitted them like a comfortable old slipper on a foot similarly shapeless, and were not the displayed, ingenious, slightly uncomfortable clothing of notions the young flaunted. There are characters in Marston's play of this kind, whether the high-born kind like Sir Lionel or Sir Hubert, or the low-born like Mulligrub. Indeed, one major distinction we shall have to consider in the play is between characters whose opinions adequately represent their inner state and those whose opinions only temporarily, or partially, or under certain circumstances represent the landscape of passion beneath. Marston, with his dramatist's ear for speech, could probably hear better than most the different quality of words rooted down through layers of acquiescence beneath, and those which had to contend with possible subterranean rebellion; and his sensitivity to such differences would surely have been sharpened immensely by a reading of Montaigne, who, as it were, constantly allows the reader to see how the surface of his mind negotiates with the matter beneath.

Among the quarter of a million people in the great city round the Inns of Court there were not only whores to attract the newcomer's attention. There was respectable citizenry also, thriving in trade, to be distinguished with a quiet upper-class smile from gentlemen born, even though they might aspire at times to that status (see III.iii.36n). And then there were thriving mulligrubs, who must often have cheated the intellectually ingenious but socially naive new young gentlemen fresh from the universities. There were the semi-educated hangers-on, the cocledemoys, 'Paul's men' who survived in a loitering life in the centre of the city (see II.i.163n).[8] And then the poor and destitute, the cast-away, those who had failed to avoid the threat of poverty that was almost as constantly present a possibility as disease (see I.i.101–9), so much so that the commonly desperate means of theft had to be countered by the ever-

[8] See Philip J. Finkelpearl, *John Marston of the Middle Temple* (Harvard University Press, 1969) p. 213, n. 27.

present gallows. And preachers everywhere threatening damnation to go with the gallows, from the fashionable pulpits of the established church as well as in the Puritan congregations and enthusiastic sects that flourished among the commercial citizenry.

The Dutch Courtesan takes the impress of this bustle of varied human life, and cannot be well understood apart from it. But, as we shall see, Marston is not only a recorder of impressions in his play; he makes of them a memorably energetic shape.

THE DYNAMIC OF THE PLAY

If *The Dutch Courtesan* were a morality play, or even the kind of play of ideas that seems to be promised by the 'argument' appended to the Prologue, then the main action would certainly present difficulties, principally the inconsistent behaviour of Freevill, who begins the play by mocking Malheureux for a sexual continence he later blames and punishes him for abandoning. But the play is not to be understood in those terms, and the argument was no doubt written in, like the tag from Martial which prefixes I.i, well after the creative energy out of which the play actually arose had ebbed. Marston in this respect was here not like Ben Jonson, the driving creative force for him was not an idea, but rather the urge to transcribe into dramatic terms the moment by moment experience of being alive, making of that transcription sudden intensities, so that the strangeness of lived human life as well as its dailiness (to use a term from Randall Jarrell) is what is presented to the audience.

Especially young human beings experience being alive, perhaps, not as a series of moments in a plot whose first three acts they already know and whose fifth act they can pretty accurately guess at, but as momentary intensities with much less before and after. This is particularly true of moments of sexual passion, which cause such a forgetting of all that came before and such a neglect of all that was planned to come after as to arouse among ponderous moralists serious disquiet. In *The Dutch Courtesan,* moral argument and moral persuasion has to contend with exactly such vivid momentary intensity, with exactly such a sense of being alive; and the play brilliantly offers the sudden new-born feel of such moments, whether the birth is fair or foul. Franceschina, for instance, rages against Freevill and curses her former lover in II.ii when she discovers his alliance with the virtuous (and pleasingly well-born and impeccably English) Beatrice. In her outsider's accents she screams for revenge:

> O Divela, life o' mine art! Ick sall be revenged! Do ten tousand hell damn me, ick sall have the rogue troat cut; and his love, and his friend, and all his

> affinity sall smart, sall die, sall hang! Now legion of divel seize him! De gran' pest, St. Anthony's fire, and de hot Neapolitan poc rot him!
> (II.ii.42–7)

Then Freevill enters with a single word:

> Franceschina!
>
> FRANCESCHINA
>
> O mine seet, dear'st, kindest, mine loving! O mine tousand, ten tousand, delicated, petty seetart! Ah, mine aderlievest affection!
> (II.ii.48–51)

This is not hypocrisy, that maintainer of a constant plan beneath a changeable surface; it is not crudely and clumsily motivated characterisation at the behest of some plot design; it is a passionate human being spinning on her axis at the possibility that the news about Beatrice was wrong, moving with a speed and a completeness and a totally unironic re-use of the linguistic energies that had raged in her an instant before that may astonish us but which also convinces us. So the 'ten tousand hell' of seconds before Freevill's entrance become the ten-tousand-fold intensity of her newly arising desire for him.

The real central action of *The Dutch Courtesan* may be seen as the struggle between the intensity of such unaffiliated moments as this and the forces which would ballast them, smooth them out to a moral consistency (whether of the virtuous Beatrice kind or the vicious Mulligrub kind), make of them a predictable, containable or useful social energy. The play is well named after its 'heroine', for it is Franceschina, the outsider in more than the ethnic sense, who is the finally untamed one, who will stay put in no category, whether moral or social, and so has to be flung aside to enable the tidy comic ending of the play.

The defining contrast with Franceschina is Beatrice. She is as anxious for Freevill's entire and undivided love as Franceschina is:

> I can some good, and, faith, I mean no hurt;
> Do not, then, sweet, wrong sober ignorance.
> I judge you all of virtue, and our vows
> Should kill all fears that base distrust can move. (II.i.23–6)

but when Freevill is unfaithful (as she thinks) she remains unchanged in her love for him. She is a fixed point as Franceschina is not, and able to be so perhaps because her reaction to love is not passionate but morally shapely. So here to Freevill, in words Franceschina would scorn:

> Dear my loved heart, be not so passionate;
> Nothing extreme lives long. (II.i.49–50)

The Dutch Courtesan is crucially concerned, we may say, with the struggle between two contending definitions of 'lives'. For Beatrice it is steady, orderly, honourable continuance inside a moral position which promises a smoothed out, rectified flow of energy. In a curious way Beatrice resembles Mary Faugh, the bawd, who has also settled to a morality which promises her long continuance, as we see when she tries to persuade Franceschina into the steadiness of being a proper whore (instead of falling in love with one of her customers), to calm her outrageous passion, at the beginning of II.ii. For Franceschina what 'lives' is, by contrast, the intense present experience, whether good or ill, whether love or revenge. The settled moral definitions which would satisfy Beatrice and Mary Faugh seem to her (as no doubt to at least some of the audience) constricting clothing for the human spirit.

If this were a kind of morality play, then the great divide would come *between* Beatrice and Mary Faugh, the question being the difference between vice and virtue as defined by the contemporary moral code (which is still largely the one our present culture acknowledges). But it is not. Instead what Marston is concerned with is the relationship between moral categorisation of any sort and the lived human experience which it has ambitions to contain. That is why Montaigne is so important to him here.

As Freevill and Malheureux debate at the beginning of the play, we are aware that they are, as it were, making speeches. That is, they are trying out the defence of freely licenced desire and the opposition case, not playfully but seriously because the life that runs within them is anxious for a moral roof to live under. In search of satisfactory habitation they both move, Freevill towards Beatrice and away from Franceschina, and Malheureux towards Franceschina and then by horrified recoil to a moral position resembling the Beatrice / Freevill domesticity. The whole drift of the play, together with the life commonly lived, both by the virtuous and the vicious, all about the three 'seeking' characters, Franceschina, Freevill and Malheureux, is towards moral categorisation, towards a settled view of life (and we may note the difference in the context of the play, for instance, between Freevill's experimental speech in favour of prostitution at I.i.98–134 and Cocledemoy's speech at I.ii.30–56; Freevill's is part of a debate with a vigorous opponent, Cocledemoy is saying just what his audience wants to hear).

In Shakespearean fashion, Marston allows his play to come to a firm conclusion (which is in favour of the morally categorised life) at the expense of the casting away of the character who has made the most indelible impression on the audience. Franceschina, refusing definition, neither bawd nor Beatrice, neither in a settled way good nor bad, is consigned to 'the extremest whip and jail' (V.iii.59). She is too dangerous for the morally shapely, for as we might well believe, if Freevill were only to say again to her at this point, as at II.ii.48: 'Franceschina!', she would swivel on her axis, love him again ten-tousand-fold and destroy the carefully built-up world of the end of the play, for that world is built of structures that, in procrustean fashion, designedly fail to answer to the moment by moment experience of being alive in favour of a mature and settled long continuance of life. Freevill and Malheureux have grown up, like their seniors in the Inns; moreover Marston himself is to be married, and will in four years be a clergyman in the Established Church.

Forget Franceschina (or perhaps that Spanish girl at the Christmas dance), forget a world where the sight of a pretty face could induce the abandonment of a whole philosophy of life in a second (so Malheureux, resembling Franceschina, at I.ii.77), forget passion. If you can.

THE PLAY IN THE THEATRE

In the preface to *The Fawn*, written shortly after *The Dutch Courtesan* (and, incidentally, celebrating uncontestedly the 'Beatrice' ideal, as does *Sophonisba*), Marston remarks that '*Comedies* are writ to be spoken, not read: Remember the life of these things consists in action'. It is by thinking of the play as a stage performance that we shall have it most vividly before us, in all its colour of contrast between high and low, virtuous and vicious, funny and terrifying, heartless and tender.

(a) The Blackfriars performance

In this relatively small, indoor theatre, before an audience largely drawn from the Inns of Court just nearby, and perhaps in the presence of the Queen, Anne of Denmark (who, according to the report of the French ambassador in 1604, especially liked coming to plays in which there was anti-Scottish satire,[9] and who set up her own household in Denmark House soon after arrival in London, the boys of her own Children of the Revels presented *The Dutch Courtesan* (entitled after another foreign woman living in London) at some point in May 1605.

It was still a summer's day outside as the play began, with the music (easily available in a choir school) that was so common a feature of plays at the Blackfriars, not only in the songs but between each act. And probably not only music, the control of what came to the ears of the audience, but some control of lighting as well would

[9] See Chambers, vol. 1, p. 325.

Reconstruction drawing of the Blackfriars theatre by C. Walter Hodges

have accompanied the three pages with lights as they came on stage to signify a night scene. There would have been, of course, plenty of boys about to allow a lavish hand with walk-on boy parts like pages, and boys as pages were in a way a good introduction to the real world *The Dutch Courtesan* is set in, the world just outside the theatre, because in that world boys were commonly pages, and here would no doubt have been familiarly dressed as such. But with the first *words* of the play a certain patina of unreality would arise to set the real world of the play apart from the real world outside, because Inns of Court men and vintners were not normally fourteen years old and with light voices. That patina of unreality would also have arisen from the words themselves. The whole of the sub-plot is conducted in a language of theatrical wit ('Nay comfort, my good host Shark'; I.i.1) which sets and displays the realism of its echo of the London streets in a kind of amber even as it portrays it. Exchanges in the taverns outside the Blackfriars were not (quite) like this fluent intensity of wit. The audience can settle to a world familiar enough for ease and far off enough for comfort. Nothing that happens in the sub-plot is going to come fully home to them. The account of Cocledemoy's deceiving of Mulligrub, especially (I.i.11–41), is a brilliant comic set-piece (almost balletic) which effectively removes both Mulligrub and Cocledemoy from audience world to stage world.

We move rapidly to a set-piece of another sort, in the exchange between Malheureux and Freevill. Here the artificiality of the case made for and against prostitution (I.i.86-162), the set speeches, would be the kind of artificiality that did actually take place outside the theatre, in the Inns of Court, so (though artificial) it is open to the real and the serious, and hovers between the earnestness of Malheureux' 'Dear my loved friend, let me be full with you' (I.i.86) and the perhaps deliberately superficial jokiness of Freevill's 'Give me my fee!' (I.i.134).

In the course of this exchange (again, we must remember, conducted between young boys) mention is first made of Franceschina, the Dutch courtesan of the title. 'I will show thee my creature' (I.i.147), Freevill says, with a certain hardness of young male ownership of a girl; but then a direct and delicate, gentle description of her:

> a pretty, nimble-eyed Dutch Tanakin; an honest, soft-hearted impropriation; a soft, plump, round-cheeked frow. (I.i.147-49)

In the next scene, we meet first Cocledemoy, who is as tough and brilliant as one might suppose from I.i.11–41, who can get his hands on money enough (I.i.11) and is a 'thick, elderly, stub-bearded fellow' (II.iii.103), a good match for the bawd, Mary

Faugh, drenched in sex as she is, and essentially unresponsive to it as she is.

This is the frame for our first view of Franceschina at I.ii.76, the picture a truly stunning contrast. The prettiest boy in the company must have played her, and boys make more convincing grown girls than grown men. Her beauty and the directness of her first words in a foreign accent must for the first time in the play fully reach the audience:

> O mine aderliver love, vat sall me do to requit dis your mush affection?
> (I.ii.81–2)

The foreignness of the accent is not comic like the wit we have so far seen in the play, not ridiculous and to be laughed at, because her beauty prevents that. It simply sets her apart from all other characters; and she will be set apart thus for the rest of the play, in a certain sense untouchable by her context, reaching for a single point of contact beyond her untouchableness (which is Freevill) and soon denied that. Throughout the play, even though her mood changes radically and violently, she is the prettiest boy on stage, and always with that isolating accent. Many men in the audience must surely have been stirred by her (if the production at the Blackfriars was any good), and even if not in agonies as Malheureux is because she is a whore (inside the play), then uneasy because she is a boy (outside the play). Part of the complaint at this time about the immorality of the theatre was that boys playing the parts of girls elicited sexual response from the men in the audience.

Freevill's confession of his morally inspired turning from this beauty (I.ii.92–4) is bracketed between her first appearance and her first song, the first set-piece of her beauty, at I.ii.115, during which time Freevill has passed her on to his friend, all unknown to her, and for high moral reasons, and surely to the at least partial indignation of an audience not in a high moral mood this afternoon at the Blackfriars. For here is the point where what I have called the dynamic of the play begins to work, the point where the play begins to be more in the minds of the audience than its brightly lit moral surface would allow. In a good production (and let us assume that the first Blackfriars production was not like the court productions of 1613)[10] the plain and direct humanity of this singing girl must sit queasily with the way she is beginning to be treated in the name of virtue. Such a dynamic divergence from the authoritative moral direction of the plot is something not to be, as it were, advertised in the programme notes, or in the official argument of the play, but rather something to be discerned here and there in the audience, as the play enacts a process amongst them. I have spoken of the pos-

[10] See p. xxix.

ition of Franceschina in the play as Shakespearean,[11] and we may have in mind perhaps something like the position of Shylock in *The Merchant of Venice*, which is a play about the satisfactory destruction of a sinister, plotting, vengeful Jew by good Christian justice; at its brightly lit surface.

The next girl to appear on stage is Beatrice. It is Freevill who sings to her in II.ii, not Franceschina to him. She is physically above him as she enters the gallery which is her window. Her beauty is delimited, not only by the courtly treatment of her by Freevill, but by the formal verse she speaks. This play is full of different 'voices' and here we have a voice of beauty very different from the singing girl of the previous scene. The next things to sing are the nightingales of II.i.65, who bring back to mind the singer of the nightingale song at I.ii.115–22, and make it not as easy as all that to dismiss Malheureux' desperate philosophising into respectability of his new passion at II.i.63–81.

Freevill amusedly contemplates Malheureux, and accurately pre-echoes at II.i.101-2 what will be Franceschina's reaction to his desertion, offering her, as it were, at this moment on the stage the caricature part of the revenging whore in which she later becomes so entangled, by the way he says the words and the laugh they no doubt get from the audience. Later in the scene, Cocledemoy has also been in Franceschina's company, together with a drunken companion, so the girl is not lacking persuaders of her real position. But her next words, at II.ii.6-8, after the audience has had an easy laugh at a bit of the sub-plot, must crucially not make them laugh:

> Grand grincome on your sentences! God's sacrament, ten tousand divels take you! You ha' brought mine love, mine honour, mine body, all to noting!

The boy playing Franceschina has here to refuse the caricature offered by Freevill. One can imagine the audience, easy from their laughter at Holifernes and Cocledemoy, and made easy by Mary Faugh's realism, beginning to laugh as Franceschina says the words predicted of her, but then stopping as she says her last sentence. If the audience can be stopped from laughing at this point, then the vengeful Franceschina of the rest of the play will always carry her humanity with her, a total humanity, not one which prefers either body or soul, but one where love is both a matter of honour and of body. Her 'ten tousand' screams out again at II.ii.43, and finally returns to Freevill at II.ii.49–50 in a way which must surely make of that now well advertised phrase something awkward and embarrassing, especially as Franceschina sings a song again a few lines later. The shapeliness of her part in the play is really striking, and it makes it difficult for an audience to reduce her to, as it were, a

[11] See p. xix.

sub-plot clown. She belongs neither to the world of the main plot nor of the sub-plot; she speaks neither in terms of high education nor of low wit. She speaks her own words, in her own foreign tongue. What is from the boys' point of view the most *assumed* accent[12] on the stage is the most direct speaking, and the character who from the point of view of common or garden realism (where everyone eventually settles into a role) is the weirdest on stage is the most nakedly human.

Franceschina's revenge plot with Malheureux reaches momentarily for caricature stage energy at II.ii.168–71 (reminding one, of course of Beatrice with Benedick in *Much Ado* IV.i), but it would be easy to prevent the audience from laughter here, so the audience are getting used to weird extremity from Franceschina which they do not easily disengage from. Malheureux twists away by the end of the scene from the isolated Franceschina, whose energy of revenge at II.ii.196–201, like her beauty, makes effective contact with nothing else on stage (though tensely making contact with the audience). Franceschina seems finally caught in her caricature role at the end of a scene where we have nevertheless been conscious of the depth of her passionate love, and so she rests until her reappearance at IV.iii, while the audience can relax into the spectacle of the shape-shifting Cocledemoy at II.iii.

Cocledemoy is as vividly himself on stage as the barber as he was as Cocledemoy, because the assuming of shapes (somewhere close to a comic version of the trying out of a moral position for life) is his native speech, is what gives him continuity (just as her virtue gives Beatrice continuity), so although in plot terms he is always turning up in unexpected guises, he is in fact totally predictable, causes the audience no difficulty as they immediately and delightedly recognise him beneath whatever disguise he has assumed. He disguises himself so easily as barber, or servant, or bellman, or pedlar, or sergeant, because he is himself by nature disguised, he lives among the fictions he creates, and so is a good story-teller in this scene.

With the beginning of Act III, a voice we have not heard before joins the throng of voices that have passed over the stage. Crispinella does not appear in Marston's source for the main plot, so in a way is his own addition to the story transformed from its sources into this play. In stage terms she is somewhere between Beatrice and Franceschina (and not beautiful, as in different ways they both are: III.i.126–7); indeed if Shakespeare's Beatrice in *Much Ado* gave her name to Freevill's chaste mistress and her 'Kill Claudio' to Franceschina, she gives her 'merry war' with Benedick

[12] Which, as Wine remarks, is actually 'a helter-skelter of Germanic, French, Italian' (p. xix, n. 15).

to Crispinella and Tysefew, as surely the audience at the Blackfriars would have recognised.

She is played by the smallest boy on stage, dressed in high shoes and a tall headpiece (III.i.109–10), which have her rather evidently striving for height, as the fashion (III.i.108) obliges, though she is not herself much worried by the shortness she thus strives in her dress to counter (III.i.106–7). The sense is here, then, of a character held within a social structure but not giving it inner allegiance, and this is true of Crispinella's overall effect in the play. She is the most Montaigne-like presence on stage (one remembers that Montaigne was, for instance, thoroughly sceptical while contriving to remain a Catholic), and perhaps the audience are meant to see her as an acceptable middle point between the naked desire of Franceschina and the imprisoning virtue of Beatrice. In fact, again in stage terms, she carefully has nothing to do with Franceschina (though notice the contrast at III.i.153–4n), does not engage with her as Beatrice does, and her effect (at times aided by a nurse deriving from Juliet's nurse in Shakespeare's play) is chiefly to emphasise the limitation of Beatrice, as she continually says things too undisguised, too 'broad' for her virtuous and modest sister (III.i.25). The marriage she will make with Tysefew (IV.i.79–83) will be outwardly conventional in a strict way, but privately free ('wanton in my bed'), and will be very different from either the union Freevill would have had with Franceschina or will have with Beatrice.

Crispinella speaks freely, then, and moves with the perhaps at times near-farcical awkwardness and care made necessary by the very little boy's high shoes and hat. Her 'disability' on stage is quite unlike Franceschina's 'disability' of speech which is not in character terms assumed as is Crispinella's dress.

After the beginning of Act III, the voices of the play are all established and functioning, and the movement of events begins increasingly to have an inevitable momentum as these forces engage with each other, the main plot and sub-plot skilfully intertwined. As any effect Franceschina can have on events is checked by the agreement between Freevill and Malheureux at the end of III.i, the rest of the act gives the audience a good stretch of sub-plot, so that by the time we reach the beginning of Act IV with the first appearance of Sir Hubert and Sir Lionel, the focus of things is decisively arranged to marginalise Franceschina. The upper-class world in all its power and fatherly authority and ignorance of naked inner life has taken a firm grasp on the action (IV.i.1–5). The banter between Crispinella and Tysefew in the rest of that scene now constitutes the outer limit of possible freedom against which to measure the relationship between Beatrice and Freevill.

When Franceschina next appears, in IV.iii, she is to be perceived as more hectic in her desperation for revenge than before; but also she is hopelessly fettered now by the plot, because she is given Freevill (disguised as Dubon, in a disguise no doubt conventionally transparent to the audience) to squire her (IV.iii.34–9), a hidden mockery of all she had hoped of his love as he becomes a kind of Cocledemoy-like grotesque to accompany her (IV.iv.33). Franceschina faces, as she comes to the end of her space in the play, not only the whoring banter of Cocledemoy and Mary Faugh but her own lover become a pander to squire her. She is almost wholly given over to her caricature role as revenging whore, but the audience, seeing the disguised Freevill, must surely remember the love she has fewer words for now but which must still sit behind her lust for revenge. Her dream of revenge is accompanied by the grotesque mutation of the lost love she revenges. That love is still vivid in her imagination as she speaks her revenge to Beatrice, saying Freevill is dead and that he loved her best:

> De yong man dat be slain did not love you, for he still lovit me ten tousant tousant times more dearly. (IV.iv.50–1)

That phrase again, so often heard, but which was Freevill's first offering to the audience of a caricature Franceschina, and which has earlier in the play carried both her revenge and her love, now carries still her almost impossible belief in Freevill's love. She knows he is slain and so can allow an uninterrupted belief that he loved her, even though he is slain by her means. The boy playing the part must have been able to make the audience remember as he said 'ten tousant tousant' (he is given the word to repeat, to make the point more effectively). Franceschina's speech here confronts Beatrice's rhetoric: 'O passion! O my grief! which way wilt break, think, and consume?' (IV.iv.53–4), so the audience can measure the complex difference between the voices.

It is Beatrice's voice which is officially preferred in the rest of this scene, her single note of self-renouncing love, not Franceschina's muddy chord of love, revenge, self-hatred; as she passes across to Beatrice her own sense of what it is to be rejected, and as an intensifier of that her own sense of her own worthlessness:

> O, but to be abused, scorned, scoffed at! O, ten tousant divla, by such a one, and unto such a one! (IV.iv.65–6)

But Franceschina, however intensely dramatic on the stage, is near the end of her time in the play. After Mulligrub is decisively cocledemoyed in IV.v, the audience again easy with the sub-plot, Malheureux is cocledemoyed by Freevill in V.i (Franceschina singing to Malheureux at V.i.17 as she had for Freevill at I.ii.115, and perhaps the same song, for she certainly echoes again her first line to Freevill; I.ii.81: V.i.18 & n). But these two survive the experience. Franceschina is cocledemoyed by Freevill after he has first tested Beatrice enough to make of her self-abnegation a thing of moral wonder and then rewarded that virtue by binding himself to it in a mutually imprisoning union. Franceschina does not survive the public tearing up of her very different union with Freevill at V.iii.33. She slips again, it would seem decisively, with almost her last words, into the caricature role prepared for her by the morally secure, on the edge of which she teeters at IV.iv.65–6. So at V.iii.42 she describes herself as 'Unprosperous divel!' and a few lines later disappears from the stage with devilish words that remind one of Iago's final silence in *Othello*. Though perhaps the boy playing the part would have said his very last word with a Dutch accent, and made it 'vill' as well as 'will', for a moment looking across the gulf of the stage to the last syllable of her love. It would need only a touch to make present again the full range of that uncategorisable figure.

The play must end very quickly now, Mulligrub released, Cocledemoy set free of the vintner's revenge, all well, the world going on, 'my very fine Heliconian gallants' (V.iii.157). Don't take it too seriously; remember the very first line of the Prologue. Of course, one often remembers what one is told to forget. Actors rely on that as they leave the stage with a graceful gesture at the triviality of what they have done.

The skill of the boys who performed in this first Blackfriars production of the play must have been far from trivial, however, and Marston must have known well what kind of dramatic demand he could make of them. The sustaining of the different voices on the stage, the registering of the flexible movement from prose to verse characteristic of the language of the play, the offering to the audience of the constant sexual innuendo, and above all perhaps the managing of the very brief moments of high intensity and significance, would all have demanded an extraordinary maturity from these boy players in a play written especially for them.[13]

(b) Later performances

Perhaps the sympathetic editor may be forgiven for imagining, as I have done, a fully adequate early performance of *The Dutch Courtesan* for the company for whom it was written and in the presence of the dramatist himself. For the subsequent stage history of the play is a melancholy one.

[13] Ann Blake comments too on the skill of these players in '"The Humour of Children": John Marston's Plays in the Private Theatres', *Review of English Studies*, new ser. 38 (1987), pp. 471–82, and on the variety they could command: 'By the time Marston's Blackfriars plays reached the stage in the years 1604–6 the company included boys, youths, and young men of seventeen at least' (p. 475).

Two performances are recorded in 1613 at court, on 25 February and 12 December, as part of the celebrations of the marriage of Princess Elizabeth to Frederick, Elector Palatine of the Rhine, in February 1613, by the adult company under her patronage, The Lady Elizabeth's Men.[14] The play was already called 'Cockle de moye' on the first of these occasions in recognition of the popularity of its sub-plot, and the fact that it was performed in celebration of a marriage must make us fairly certain that the other dominant feature of the performances was the Beatrice / Freevill union. The centrality of the decisively defeated Franceschina, so vital to the knife-edge acuity of the balance of the forces in the play, would probably have been lost amid brilliant low-life farce and solemn high-life idealisation.

The unaffiliated Franceschina holds the play together, and it is hardly surprising that as the importance of her part declined the play should begin to fall apart. The change of title in 1613 is already significant (we should hope little from an *Othello* retitled *Desdemona, or The Virtuous Wife Reveng'd*), and by the time the theatres were closed in 1642 the sub-plot was independently popular enough to be played during the interregnum as a separate 'droll' called *The Cheater Cheated.*[15]

With the Restoration, the entire play was adapted by Aphra Behn as *The Revenge, or A Match in Newgate* (1680),[16] tidied into sentimentalised triviality, and this provided the basis for Christopher Bullock's *A Woman's Revenge, or A Match in Newgate* (1715) and his 'ballad-opera' *Love and Revenge, or The Vintner Outwitted* (1729). The sub-plot, disentangled from the mangled remnants of Marston's play, survived in various forms for the rest of the eighteenth century.[17]

The original play was given a fresh chance by Joan Littlewood at the Theatre Workshop in Stratford East in February 1954, and again in April 1959. The critical reaction was mixed, but *The Times* reviewer noted of the 1954 production that Avis Bunnage played Franceschina 'as a real woman and not a stage slut' and described the whole production as 'imaginative and often beautiful'.[18] Again, there was a National Theatre production in 1964, directed by William Gaskell and Piers Haggard, which although not very well received by some of the critics, both made very funny business of

[14] Chambers, vol. 3, p. 431; vol. 4, pp. 180, 182.

[15] See Francis Kirkman's collection of 'drols and farces', *The Wits, or Sport upon Sport* (1673), ed. John James Elson (New York, 1932) pp. 346–67.

[16] On the authorship of this adaptation, see Scott, pp. 124–5, n. 18.

[17] For a more detailed account of these adaptations, see Scott, pp. 104–7, and Hughes and Scouten, pp. 98–114.

[18] *The Times* 24 February 1954; and see Scott, p. 111.

the sub-plot and allowed Franceschina genuine status, while emphasising the strangeness of the male sexual attitudes in the play. An Off Off-Broadway production took place at the Casa Italiana Renaissance Theatre in New York in 1966; and more recently, the 1990 production at The Man in the Moon Theatre in London by Vivienne Cottrell was enthusiastically noted by Katherine Duncan-Jones,[19] who suggested that *The Dutch Courtesan* is a play which would repay imaginative thought in modern productions. Perhaps its day has come round again at last.

THE TEXT

The Dutch Courtesan was entered in the Stationers' Register on 26 June 1605 and published in quarto in the same year. A copy of the quarto, printed by T[homas] P[urfoot] for John Hodgets, now in the Bodleian Library (shelfmark: Malone 252(5)), provides the copy text for the present edition. It seems likely that the quarto was set from manuscript copy prepared by the author for the press: a list of *dramatis personae* is provided, which is unusual in theatrical manuscripts of the time; the descriptive stage directions show evidence of authorial care rather than the concerns of the prompt book; and the play begins with a Latin tag that can have been no part of its performance on stage, but has been clearly inserted for the printed version.

The 1605 quarto (Q) exists in both corrected and uncorrected states in its twelve extant copies, all of which have been collated by M. L. Wine (Regents Renaissance Drama Series, Arnold, 1965) and Peter Davison (Oliver & Boyd, 1968). The only other printing of the play in Marston's lifetime was in a collection of six of his plays published without his authorisation by William Sheares in 1633. Cancels obliterating the name of the author in the second issue of this volume seem plainly at Marston's own demand, and the 1633 text has as a consequence no substantive authority, although it does at times produce readings which I accept as clarifying a difficulty in Q. Readings are also occasionally accepted from a state of Q, either corrected (c) or uncorrected (u), not represented by the Bodleian copy. Emendations accepted from any later edition of the play are marked 'ed.' in the textual notes.

All departures from the copy text are recorded in the textual notes, except that spelling and punctuation have been silently modernised; act and scene divisions and stage directions or portions of stage directions simply supplied from previous editions of the play, with no emendation of Q, are put in the square brackets which denote departures from Q outside the spoken text proper, but with no textual note.

[19] *Times Literary Supplement* 23 February–1 March 1990.

FURTHER READING

The list of abbreviations provides information about other modern editions of *The Dutch Courtesan*, and the selection of Marston's plays by Jackson and Neill can be particularly recommended as making easily accessible the best of his work.

The development of critical attitudes to Marston in the twentieth century can be traced by beginning with T. S. Eliot's essay first published in his *Elizabethan Essays* (London, 1934). It may fairly be said that Eliot is grudging about Marston's achievement, and the difficulty critics have had with him as well as recognition of his strange strengths characterise much subsequent critical writing. Una Ellis-Fermor writes on him in *The Jacobean Drama* (London, 1936), and Samuel Schoenbaum is fascinated by 'The Precarious Balance of John Marston', *Publications of the Modern Language Association of America*, 67 (1952), pp. 1069–78. Other studies are by G. K. Hunter, 'English Folly and Italian Vice', in *Jacobean Theatre*, ed. John Russell Brown and Bernard Harris (London, 1960) and Anthony Caputi, *John Marston, Satirist* (Cornell University Press, 1961). R. A. Foakes writes sympathetically in *Shakespeare: The Dark Comedies to the Last Plays: from Satire to Celebration* (London, 1971) and more recent studies include Michael Scott, *John Marston's Plays: Theme, Structure and Performance* (London, 1978), George L. Geckle, *John Marston's Drama: Themes, Images, Sources* (Farleigh Dickinson University Press, 1980) and T. F. Wharton, *The Critical Fall and Rise of John Marston* (Camden House, 1994).

The best and most elaborate attempt to place Marston in his context and understand him in terms of it is by Philip J. Finkelpearl, *John Marston of the Middle Temple* (Harvard University Press, 1969), and there are two more recent studies on the theatrical context of the boys' companies for which he wrote by Michael Shapiro, *Children of the Revels* (Columbia University Press, 1977) and Reavley Gair, *The Children of Paul's: The Story of a Theatre Company* (Cambridge University Press, 1982).

Title page from 1605 edition, shelfmark *Mal.252(5)*, Bodleian Library, University of Oxford.

THE
Dutch Courtezan.

AS

IT WAS PLAYD IN THE
Blacke-Friars, by the Children
of her Maiesties Reuels.

VVritten
BY IOHN MARSTON.

AT LONDON,
¶ Printed by T. P. for *Iohn Hodgets*,
and are to be sould at his shop in
Paules Church-yard. 1605.

PROLOGUE

Slight hasty labours in this easy play,
Present not what you would, but what we may:
For this vouchsafe to know, the only end
Of our now study is, not to offend.
Yet think not but, like others, rail we could,
(Best art presents, not what it can, but should)
And if our pen in this seem over slight,
We strive not to instruct, but to delight.
As for some few we know of purpose here
To tax and scout: know firm art cannot fear
Vain rage: only the highest grace we pray
Is, you'll not tax until you judge our play.
Think, and then speak: 'tis rashness, and not wit,
To speak what is in passion, and not judgement, fit.
Sit then, with fair expectance, and survey
Nothing but passionate man in his slight play,
Who hath this only ill – to some deemed worst –
A modest diffidence and self-mistrust.

FABULAE ARGUMENTUM

The difference betwixt the love of a courtesan and a wife is the full scope of the play, which, intermixed with the deceits of a witty city jester, fills up the comedy.

1 *easy* easily written (See 8n.)

3–5 *the only . . . could* 'Possibly a backward glance at the Theatre War in which Marston and Jonson were ranged on opposite sides' (Davison).

4 *now* present

8 Marston here rejects the Horatian (and Jonsonian) ideal that art should both please and instruct. Jonson replied to this attack in the preface to *Volpone* (1606), where he also rebuts the charge that he wrote laboriously and slowly (by contrast with Marston). But see also V.ii.75.

10 *tax and scout* censure and scornfully reject

15 *expectance* expectation

16 *passionate man* i.e. Malheureux
his i.e. Marston's (though conceivably also Malheureux', in which case 'play' would take on too a slightly metaphorical sense)

FABULAE ARGUMENTUM The Argument of the Play

FRANCESCHINA ed. (Francischina Q) 'name of the flirtatious serving-maid in the Italian *commedia dell'arte*' (Jackson and Neill).

MARY FAUGH 'Marry, faugh!' was a common expression of disgust.

BEATRICE See II.ii.165–70n.

CRISPINELLA from *crispus* (Lat. = curly-haired), but with a glance at the brisk, decisive quality of 'crisp'.

PUTIFER from *putiferio* (It. = stench)

TYSEFEW ?from *tisonner* + *feu* (Fr. = to poke the fire + fire)

CAQUETEUR from *caqueter* (Fr. = to chatter)

MALHEUREUX (Fr. = unfortunate, unhappy, wretched). See V.ii.96.

COCLEDEMOY OED cites a single instance of 'cockle-demois', from Chapman's Inns of Court masque of 1613, where it seems to mean 'shells of some kind representing money'; perhaps that sense of the counterfeit or the worthless goes together here with a pun on 'cuckold + *moi*'.

MULLIGRUB The 'money-grubbing' vintner ends with a fit of the 'mulligrubs' (= depression, colic).

REINSCURE from 'reins' (= kidneys, loins). See II.i.171.

PAGES . . . OFFICERS (*not in* Q)

DRAMATIS PERSONAE

FRANCESCHINA	*a Dutch courtesan*
MARY FAUGH	*an old woman*
SIR LIONEL FREEVILL SIR HUBERT SUBBOYS	*two old knights*
YOUNG FREEVILL	*Sir Lionel's son*
BEATRICE CRISPINELLA	*Sir Hubert's daughters*
PUTIFER	*their nurse*
TYSEFEW	*a blunt gallant*
CAQUETEUR	*a prattling gull*
MALHEUREUX	*young Freevill's unhappy friend*
COCLEDEMOY	*a knavishly witty City companion*
MASTER MULLIGRUB	*a vintner*
MISTRESS MULLIGRUB	*his wife*
MASTER BURNISH	*a goldsmith*
LIONEL	*his man*
HOLIFERNES REINSCURE	*a barber's boy*
THREE WATCHMEN [CONSTABLES]	
[PAGES	
LADIES	
GENTLEMEN	
ROGER	
CHRISTIAN	
SERVANTS	
OFFICERS]	

Turpe . . . nugas (printed in right-hand margin below title Q)
'It is discreditable to have (as a profession the writing of) trivial stuff which is also difficult (to compose).' This line from Martial (*Epigrammata* II.lxxxvi.9) only makes complete sense when taken with the following: *Et stultus labor est ineptiarum* (= and to labour at absurd things is foolish). See Introduction, p. xxxi and Prologue 8n.

THE DUTCH COURTESAN

Turpe est difficiles habere nugas

Act I, Scene i

Enter three Pages with lights, MULLIGRUB, FREEVILL, MALHEUREUX, TYSEFEW, *and* CAQUETEUR

FREEVILL

Nay comfort, my good host Shark, my good Mulligrub.

MALHEUREUX

Advance thy snout; do not suffer thy sorrowful nose to drop on thy Spanish leather jerkin, most hardly honest Mulligrub.

FREEVILL

What, cogging Cocledemoy is run away with a nest of goblets? True, what then? They will be hammered out well enough, I warrant you.

MULLIGRUB

Sure, some wise man would find them out presently.

FREEVILL

Yes, sure, if we could find out some wise man presently.

MALHEUREUX

How was the plate lost? How did it vanish?

0 s.d.1 *with lights* The carrying of torches is a conventional indication of a night scene

1 *Shark* Swindler

3 *Spanish leather* the most expensive kind
hardly honest The word 'hardly' is surely intended to veer ironically away from its near neighbour in sound 'hardy'.

5 *cogging* cheating

5–6 *nest of goblets* set of goblets fitting one inside the other

6 *hammered out* flattened with a hammer so that they could be sold for the value of the metal and not identified, with a glance at the sense of 'hammer out' as meaning 'devise a means' (OED Hammer v 2a): a means of disposing of them will have been rapidly contrived

8 *presently* immediately, at once

9 *wise man* Freevill uses the phrase in its usual sense, but Mulligrub really has a wizard in mind in the previous line; he is certainly prepared to resort to magic at III.iii.104–5.

FREEVILL

In most sincere prose, thus: that man of much money, some wit, but less honesty, cogging Cocledemoy, comes this night late into mine host's Mulligrub's tavern here, calls for a room. The house being full, Cocledemoy, consorted with his movable chattel, his instrument of fornication, the bawd Mistress Mary Faugh, are imparloured next the street. Good poultry was their food: blackbird, lark, woodcock; and mine host here comes in, cries 'God bless you!' and departs. A blind harper enters, craves audience, uncaseth, plays. The drawer, for female privateness' sake, is nodded out, who, knowing that whosoever will hit the mark of profit must, like those that shoot in stone-bows, wink with one eye, grows blind o'th' right side and departs.

CAQUETEUR

He shall answer for that winking with one eye at the last day.

MALHEUREUX

Let him have day till then, and he will wink with both his eyes.

FREEVILL

Cocledemoy, perceiving none in the room but the blind harper (whose eyes heaven had shut up from beholding wickedness), unclasps a casement to the street very patiently, pockets up three bowls unnaturally, thrusts his wench forth the window, and himself most preposterously, with his heels forward, follows. The unseeing harper plays

13 *host's* ed. (hostes Q)

14 *Cocledemoy,* ed. (∼‸ Q)

14–15 *consorted with* (sexually) together with

16–17 *imparloured . . . street* i.e. had a private room at street level instead of upstairs

20 *uncaseth* takes his (small Elizabethan) harp from its case
drawer tapster

21 *nodded out* dismissed with a nod of the head

22 *stone-bows* a kind of crossbow or catapult used for shooting stones

23 *wink with* close
o'th' right side in the right eye, i.e. (with a pun) to what is right (by condoning fornication)

27 *have day* postpone payment, i.e. postpone his damnation

30 *from beholding* so that he did not see

33 *forth* out of
preposterously In the literal sense, after (post) side, before (pre), instead of putting a head out of the window.

on, bids the empty dishes and the treacherous candles much good do them. The drawer returns; but, out alas, not only the birds, but also the nest of goblets were flown away. Laments are raised, –

TYSEFEW

Which did not pierce the heavens.

FREEVILL

The drawers moan, mine host doth cry, the bowls are gone.

MULLIGRUB

Hic finis Priami!

MALHEUREUX

Nay, be not jaw-fallen, my most sharking Mulligrub.

FREEVILL

'Tis your just affliction. Remember the sins of the cellar, and repent, repent!

MULLIGRUB

I am not jaw-fallen, but I will hang the cony-catching Cocledemoy, and there's an end of't. *Exit*

CAQUETEUR

[*to Tysefew*] Is it a right stone? It shows well by candlelight.

[TYSEFEW]

So do many things that are counterfeit, but I assure you this is a right diamond.

CAQUETEUR

Might I borrow it of you? It will not a little grace my finger in visitation of my mistress.

[TYSEFEW]

Why, use it, most sweet Caqueteur, use it.

35–6 *bids . . . them* Having no reward from the empty room for his playing, he irritably wishes 'much good may your lack of generosity do you' to the audience of diners he thinks he has.

39 i.e. heaven made no reply

41 Here was Priam's end. Mulligrub slightly misquotes Vergil (*Aeneid* II.554) as he compares the tragedy which has befallen him with the slaying of Priam, King of Troy.

43 *cellar* ed. (sellar Q). Mulligrub sins in his wine-cellar in the way Cocledemoy describes at V.iii.102–13.

45 *cony-catching* cheating

48 s.p. ed. (*Free.* Q). We know from III.i.142–3 that Caqueteur borrowed a diamond from Tysefew, hence the emended speech headings here and at 52.

49 *right* genuine

51 *visitation of* visiting

52 s.p. ed. (*Free.* Q)

CAQUETEUR

Thanks, good sir. [*to the others*] 'Tis grown high night. Gentles, rest to you.

Exit, [*his Page lighting him*]

TYSEFEW

A torch! – Sound wench, soft sleep, and sanguine dreams to you both. – On, boy!

[*Exit, his Page lighting him*]

FREEVILL

[*going*] Let me bid you good rest.

MALHEUREUX

Not so, trust me, I must bring my friend home; I dare not give you up to your own company; I fear the warmth of wine and youth will draw you to some common house of lascivious entertainment.

FREEVILL

Most necessary buildings, Malheureux. Ever since my intention of marriage, I do pray for their continuance.

MALHEUREUX

Loved sir, your reason?

FREEVILL

Marry, lest my house should be made one. I would have married men love the stews as Englishmen love the Low Countries: wish war should be maintained there lest it should come home to their own doors. What, suffer a man to have a hole to put his head in, though he go to the pillory for it. Youth and appetite are above the club of Hercules.

53 *high* deep 54 s.d. *his . . . him* (*not in* Q)

55 *Sound* Healthy, free of the pox

56 s.d. (*not in* Q)

57 s.d. (*not in* Q)

66 *love* 1633 (lou'd Q)

66–7 *Low Countries* Netherlands; but also a sexual reference to the 'low' parts of women, below the waist (cf. the description of the kitchen-wench in *The Comedy of Errors* III.ii). Elizabethan policy was to support the Dutch fighting against the Spanish in the Netherlands, so that Spain should not attack England.

69 *hole . . . in* shelter to go to, though the sexual innuendo is the main point here; for 'hole' and 'head' read vagina and penis, which might bring a man to the real hole and head of a pillory

70–1 *above . . . Hercules* i.e. beyond restraint even by the greatest possible force, though 'ironically, Hercules symbolised sexual potency as well as strength and virtue' (Davison), and if, as we well may, we take 'club' as allowing a sexual innuendo, then youth and appetite outstrip rather than defy Hercules

MALHEUREUX
This lust is a most deadly sin, sure.
FREEVILL
Nay, 'tis a most lively sin, sure.
MALHEUREUX
Well, I am sure 'tis one of the head sins.
FREEVILL
Nay, I am sure it is one of the middle sins.
MALHEUREUX
Pity, 'tis grown a most daily vice.
FREEVILL
But a more nightly vice, I assure you.
MALHEUREUX
Well, 'tis a sin.
FREEVILL
Ay, or else few men would wish to go to heaven: and, not to disguise with my friend, I am now going the way of all flesh.
MALHEUREUX
Not to a courtesan?
FREEVILL
A courteous one.
MALHEUREUX
What, to a sinner?
FREEVILL
A very publican.
MALHEUREUX
Dear my loved friend, let me be full with you.
Know, sir, the strongest argument that speaks
Against the soul's eternity is lust,
That wise man's folly and the fool's wisdom.
But to grow wild in loose lasciviousness,

74 *head sins* capital sins; sins committed by the 'head' or penis (though Malheureux no doubt does not intend the *double entendre*)

75 *middle sins* sins committed in the middle of the body

79 *or . . . heaven* i.e. if it were not a sin, most men would be satisfied with (sexual) life on earth and not wish for heaven

80–1 *the . . . flesh* This is normally to death, but here the 'death' of orgasm.

83 Freevill corrects Malheureux' disapproval with what would have been in seventeenth-century pronunciation an easy chime with 'courtesan'.

85 *publican* i.e. a public one, a public sinner; but with also the chastening reminder that Christ consorted with 'publicans and sinners'

86 *full* unrestrainedly honest

88 *Against . . . eternity* '*Alexander* said, that he knew himself mortall chiefly by this [sexual] action, and by sleeping' (Montaigne III.v.126).

Given up to heat and sensual appetite,
Nay, to expose your health and strength and name,
Your precious time, and with that time the hope
Of due preferment, advantageous means
Of any worthy end, to the stale use,
The common bosom, of a money-creature,
One that sells human flesh, a mangonist!

FREEVILL

Alas, good creatures, what would you have them do? Would you have them get their living by the curse of man, the sweat of their brows? So they do. Every man must follow his trade, and every woman her occupation. A poor, decayed mechanical man's wife, her husband is laid up; may not she lawfully be laid down when her husband's only rising is by his wife's falling? A captain's wife wants means, her commander lies in open field abroad; may not she lie in civil arms at home? A waiting gentlewoman, that had wont to take say to her lady, miscarries or so; the court misfortune throws her down; may not the city courtesy take her up? Do you know no alderman would pity such a woman's case? Why, is charity grown a sin? or relieving the poor and impotent an offence? You will say beasts take no money for their fleshly entertainment. True, because they are beasts, therefore beastly. Only men give to loose, because they are men, therefore manly; and, indeed, wherein should they bestow their money better? In land, the title

91 *heat* passion
95 *stale* worn, the worse for use
97 *mangonist* furbisher up of inferior wares for sale
99–100 *curse . . . do* After the Fall, human kind was condemned to such sweating labour (Genesis 3.19), and the whore dutifully sweats during copulation.
101 *occupation* Elizabethan slang for sexual activity
102 *mechanical man* manual labourer, craftsman, artisan
106 *civil arms* the arms of a civilian (as distinct from the soldier husband), with a glance at 'civil' in the sense 'obliging'
107 *take say* sample food and drink before presenting it (OED Say sb[2] 7), in this case clearly her mistress' lovers, by whom she falls pregnant
or so as it were, let us say
110 *case* situation; vagina
111 *poor and impotent* The poor may be the unfortunate women, forced to such shifts by their helplessness (impotence), but the impotence may also be on the part of their husbands, who are assisted in the performance of their part by the adulterer.
113 *give to loose* 'give money that they might (a) live loosely, (b) lose all they have, financially and sexually' (Davison)

may be cracked; in houses, they may be burnt; in apparel, 'twill wear; in wine, alas for pity, our throat is but short. But employ your money upon women, and, a thousand to nothing, some one of them will bestow that on you which shall stick by you as long as you live. They are no ingrateful persons; they will give *quid* for *quo*: do ye protest, they'll swear; do you rise, they'll fall; do you fall, they'll rise; do you give them the French crown, they'll give you the French – *O iustus iusta iustum!* They sell their bodies; do not better persons sell their souls? Nay, since all things have been sold – honour, justice, faith – nay, even God himself:

Ay me, what base ignobleness is it
To sell the pleasure of a wanton bed?
Why do men scrape, why heap to full heaps join?
But for his mistress, who would care for coin?
For this I hold to be denied of no man:
All things are made for man, and man for woman.
Give me my fee!

MALHEUREUX

Of ill you merit well. My heart's good friend,
Leave yet at length, at length; for know this ever:
'Tis no such sin to err, but to persever.

FREEVILL

Beauty is woman's virtue, love the life's music, and

116 *cracked* flawed
117 *throat . . . short* appetite for drink soon sated
121 *quid* ed. (quite Q)
quid for quo i.e. *quid pro quo* (tit for tat)
123–4 *give them . . . French –* in return for the coin of payment (and 'the French crown' was also a slang term for the baldness brought on by syphilis) they will give you the French pox
124 *O . . . iustum* O just, just, just (the Latin word in all three nominative forms for emphasis)
They . . . bodies '[Prostitutes] *sell but their bodyes, their willes cannot be put to sale;* that is too free, and too much it's owne' (Montaigne III.v.132).
128 *what . . . it* i.e. why should it be thought base and ignoble?
128–9 ed. (*as prose* Q)
130 *scrape* amass (wealth)
133–4 1633 (*as one line* Q)
134 i.e. give me my lawyer's fee in return for my speech in defence of whores
136 *yet at length* now at last
138 *Beauty . . . virtue 'Beautie is the true availefull advantage of women'* (Montaigne III.iii.52).

woman the dainties or second course of heaven's curious workmanship. Since, then, beauty, love, and woman are good, how can the love of woman's beauty be bad? And *bonum, quo communius, eo melius.* Wilt, then, go with me?

MALHEUREUX

Whither?

FREEVILL

To a house of salvation.

MALHEUREUX

Salvation?

FREEVILL

Yes, 'twill make thee repent. Wilt go to the Family of Love? I will show thee my creature: a pretty, nimble-eyed Dutch Tanakin; an honest, soft-hearted impropriation; a soft, plump, round-cheeked frow, that has beauty enough for her virtue, virtue enough for a woman, and woman enough for any reasonable man in my knowledge. Wilt pass along with me?

MALHEUREUX

What, to a brothel? to behold an impudent prostitution? Fie on't! I shall hate the whole sex to see her. The most odious spectacle the earth can present is an immodest, vulgar woman.

FREEVILL

Good, still; my brain shall keep't. You must go as you love me.

MALHEUREUX

Well, I'll go to make her loathe the shame she's in.
The sight of vice augments the hate of sin.

139 *dainties* 1633 (daintines Q)
the ... course created second, after man, they are the sweets to follow the main dish
curious careful, ingenious

142 *bonum ... melius* the more widely shared a good is, the better

146–7 *Family of Love* Millenarian originally Dutch sect supposed to practise free love (to which the Mulligrubs belong; see III.iii.49–51), the religious reference is here used to mean a brothel, which is the use Mary Faugh makes of it at I.ii.17–18.

148 *Tanakin* diminutive form of Ann or Anna used for a Dutch or German girl
impropriation property of (usually a religious, and not as here a bawdy) house

149 *frow* Dutchwoman

153 *prostitution* prostitute (the long form of the word perhaps used to match and counter Freevill's 'impropriation')

157 *Good ... keep't* i.e. yet another good saying (referring to Malheureux' last sentence); I'll remember it

FREEVILL

'The sight of vice augments the hate of sin.' Very fine, perdy!

Exeunt, [*the Page lighting them*]

Act I, Scene ii

Enter COCLEDEMOY *and* MARY FAUGH

COCLEDEMOY

Mary, Mary Faugh!

MARY FAUGH

Hem!

COCLEDEMOY

Come, my worshipful, rotten, rough-bellied bawd! Ha, my blue-toothed patroness of natural wickedness, give me the goblets.

MARY FAUGH

By yea and by nay, Master Cocledemoy, I fear you'll play the knave and restore them.

COCLEDEMOY

No, by the Lord, aunt, restitution is Catholic, and thou knowest we love –

MARY FAUGH

What?

COCLEDEMOY

Oracles are ceased; *tempus praeteritum.* Dost hear, my wor-

162 *perdy* by God

162 s.d. *the . . . them* (*not in* Q)

4 *blue-toothed* i.e. with rotten teeth

8 *aunt* bawd

restitution is Catholic The Catholic pastoral practice was generally to make sacramental absolution dependent upon restitution or reparation on the part of the penitent. Among Protestants, the doctrine of election did away with the mechanisms of sacramental remission of sin, this part included, especially in extreme sects like the Mulligrub's Family of Love (see I.i.146–7n) where predestinarian notions of God's grace were strong and where in addition perhaps ideas about community of property prevailed. The Catholic faith was forbidden in England at this time.

10 *What?* The word missing as Mary Faugh interrupts is probably 'grace'. She is mockingly incredulous at Cocledemoy's Protestant mock-piety, and in return in his reply he calls her a merely pagan bawd, to which she wittily responds by asserting her impeccably extreme Protestant Christain credentials.

11 *tempus praeteritum* time (is) past, i.e. remember that with the advent of Christianity, the pagan age of oracles is past history

shipful clyster-pipe, thou ungodly fire that burnt Diana's temple? Dost hear, bawd?

MARY FAUGH

In very good truthness, you are the foulest-mouthed, profane, railing brother! Call a woman the most ungodly names! I must confess we all eat of the forbidden fruit; and, for mine own part, though I am one of the Family of Love and, as they say, a bawd that covers the multitude of sins, yet I trust I am none of the wicked that eat fish o' Fridays.

COCLEDEMOY

Hang toasts! I rail at thee, my worshipful organ-bellows that fills the pipes, my fine rattling, phlegmy cough o' the lungs and cold with a pox? I rail at thee? What, my right precious pandress, supportress of barber-surgeons and enhanceress of lotium and diet-drink! I rail at thee, necessary

12 *clyster-pipe* tube for administering suppositories, i.e. the bawd is the means whereby the customer enters the whore. See 102.

12–13 *ungodly . . . temple* Mary Faugh is given the part of Herostratus, who burnt down the temple of Diana, goddess of chastity, in 356 B.C.

14 *truthness* truth

15 *brother* term of address to a fellow (male) member of a Protestant sect

16 *eat . . . fruit* i.e. sin like Eve

17–19 *though . . . sins* Mary Faugh lightly asserts her membership of the Mulligrub's sect in order to convert 'Family of Love' immediately to her own bawdy purposes and put herself in the place of Christ who for a predestinarian Protestant covers the sins of the elect, concealing them from the judging eye of God the Father. See also I Peter 4.8.

19–20 *yet . . . Fridays* Catholics used to eat fish on Fridays because forbidden on that day to eat meat. A convinced Protestant would judge the Catholic faith as wicked. Mary Faugh trusts that at any rate she is not a Catholic even though she is of the 'family of love'; that concessive force would not have been appropriate if she really had been of this sect; the phrasing then would have been 'I am of the Family of Love and not one of the wicked'. See 8n.

21 *Hang toasts* Cocledemoy's favourite exclamation. Small pieces of spiced toast were often dropped into wine. Perhaps the oath means that wine is best unadulterated with fussy spices.

21–2 *organ-bellows . . . pipes* The pox (= syphilis) gave one cold symptoms in the windpipes, the pipes filled with catarrh suggest organ pipes filled with air, the organ-bellows suggest inflation of the male organ by what is offered by a bawd.

24 *barber-surgeons* i.e. medical practitioners

24–5 *enhanceress* ed. (inhauntres Q) i.e. raiser of the price

25 *lotium* stale urine, used by barbers as a treatment for the hair loss occasioned by the pox (see I.i.123–4n)
diet-drink medicinal potion (to 'take diet' was to be treated for the pox)

25–6 *necessary damnation* both a damned soul and the bringer of damnation, 'necessary' because sex is necessary

damnation? I'll make an oration, I, in praise of thy most courtly-in-fashion and most pleasurable function, I.

MARY FAUGH

I prithee do. I love to hear myself praised, as well as any old lady, I.

COCLEDEMOY

List, then; a bawd: first for her profession or vocation, it is most worshipful of all the twelve companies; for as that trade is most honourable that sells the best commodities – as the draper is more worshipful than the pointmaker, the silkman more worshipful than the draper, and the goldsmith more honourable than both, little Mary – so the bawd above all. Her shop has the best ware, for where these sell but cloth, satins, and jewels, she sells divine virtues, as virginity, modesty, and such rare gems, and those not like a petty chapman, by retail, but like a great merchant, by wholesale. Wa, ha, ho! And who are her customers? Not base corn-cutters or sow-gelders, but most rare wealthy knights and most rare bountiful lords are her customers. Again, whereas no trade or vocation profiteth but by the loss and displeasure of another – as the merchant thrives not but by the licentiousness of giddy and unsettled youth, the lawyer but by the vexation of his client, the physician but by the maladies of his patient – only my smooth-gummed bawd lives by others' pleasure, and only grows rich by others' rising. O merciful gain! O righteous income! So much for her vocation, trade, and life. As for their death, how can it be bad since their wickedness is always before their eyes, and a death's head

31 *twelve companies* the twelve major London livery companies

33 *draper* maker of woollen cloth
pointmaker maker of laces for fastening clothes (pointmakers were not among the twelve companies)

34 *silkman* i.e. mercer

39 *petty chapman* small trader

40 *by* 1633 (hy Q)
Wa, ha, ho cry of the falconer to lure the falcon. See also 133.

41 *corn-cutters* chiropodists

44–7 *the merchant . . . client* 'The Merchant thrives not but by the licentiousnesse of youth ... the Lawyer by suits and controversies betweene men' (Montaigne I.xxi.112)

48 *smooth-gummed* Because of having lost her teeth to the pox.

49 *rising* with a *double entendre* referring to erection

50 *income* with a *double entendre* referring to the man's ejaculation into the woman

52–3 *and a . . . finger* A ring with a death's head on it would commonly be worn by a bawd.

most commonly on their middle finger? To conclude, 'tis most certain they must needs both live well and die well, since most commonly they live in Clerkenwell and die in Bridewell. *Dixi*, Mary.

Enter FREEVILL *and* MALHEUREUX, [*preceded by a Page with a light*]

FREEVILL

Come along; yonder's the preface or exordium to my wench, the bawd. – Fetch, fetch!

[*Exit* MARY FAUGH]

What, Master Cocledemoy! Is your knaveship yet stirring? Look to it, Mulligrub lies for you.

COCLEDEMOY

The more fool he; I can lie for myself, worshipful friend. Hang toasts! I vanish? Ha, my fine boy, thou art a scholar and hast read Tully's *Offices*, my fine knave. Hang toasts!

FREEVILL

The vintner will toast you and he catch you.

COCLEDEMOY

I will draw the vintner to the stoup, and when he runs low, tilt him. Ha, my fine knave, art going to thy recreation?

FREEVILL

Yes, my capricious rascal.

COCLEDEMOY

Thou wilt look like a fool, then, by and by.

FREEVILL

Look like a fool? Why?

55 *Clerkenwell* District in London famous as a haunt of whores.

56 *Bridewell* A London prison.
Dixi I have spoken, i.e. that is my case, the formal end of an oration in classical Rome

59 *stirring* abroad, not in hiding

60 *in* Q *a mistaken s.d. 'Enter Cocledemoy.' precedes this line*
lies lies in wait

63 *Tully's Offices* Cicero's *De Officiis*, in which he sets out a practical code of behaviour for his son. It was the best known work of moral philosophy at this time. See II.i.163n.

64 *and* if

65–6 *vintner . . . him* The vintner's flagon ('stoup'), part of his usual equipment, becomes punningly a stooping low, and as he runs along low (in another sense than the vintner's usual running low in supplies of drink), he is easily tripped up, or tilted over, as his cask would be tilted to pour out its last drops.

67 *capricious* sure-footed in wit, like the goat (Lat. *capra*) from which the word comes, and with a glance no doubt at the reputation of the goat for lechery

COCLEDEMOY

Why, according to the old saying, a beggar when he is lousing of himself looks like a philosopher, a hard-bound philosopher when he is on the stool looks like a tyrant, and a wise man when he is in his belly-act looks like a fool. God give your worship good rest! Grace and mercy keep your syringe straight and your lotium unspilt! [*Exit*]

Enter FRANCESCHINA

FREEVILL

See, sir, this is she.

MALHEUREUX

This?

FREEVILL

This. [*kissing her*]

MALHEUREUX

A courtesan? [*Aside*] Now cold blood defend me! What a proportion afflicts me!

FRANCESCHINA

O mine aderliver love, vat sall me do to requit dis your mush affection?

FREEVILL

Marry, salute my friend, clip his neck, and kiss him welcome.

FRANCESCHINA

O' mine art, sir, you bin very velcome. [*kissing Malheureux*]

FREEVILL

Kiss her, man, with a more familiar affection. [*Malheureux kisses her*] So. – Come, what entertainment? Go to your lute.

Exit FRANCESCHINA

71 *hard-bound* constipated

73 *belly-act* copulation

75 *syringe . . . unspilt* Cocledemoy wishes him metaphorically a good erection and no premature ejaculation.

78 s.d. (*not in* Q)

79 *A courtesan?* i.e. is so beautiful a girl as this a whore?

79–80 *What . . . me* Malheureux has just wished for an access of cold blood to stem the rapid change in the equable proportioning of his humours made by his sudden hot-blooded lust; but perhaps the more obvious change of proportion he would be afflicted with is a physical erection.

81 *aderliver* Franceschina's English version of the Dutch alderliefest = dearest *requit* requite

85 *art* heart

85 s.d. (*not in* Q)

86–7 s.d. (*not in* Q)

– And how dost approve my sometimes elected? She's none of your ramping cannibals that devour man's flesh, nor any of your Curtian gulfs that will never be satisfied until the best thing a man has be thrown into them. I loved her with my heart until my soul showed me the imperfection of my body, and placed my affection on a lawful love, my modest Beatrice, which if this short-heels knew, there were no being for me with eyes before her face. But, faith, dost thou not somewhat excuse my sometimes incontinency with her enforcive beauties? Speak!

MALHEUREUX

Ha, she is a whore, is she not?

FREEVILL

Whore? Fie, whore! You may call her a courtesan, a cockatrice, or (as that worthy spirit of an eternal happiness said) a suppository. But whore, fie! 'Tis not in fashion to call things by their right names. Is a great merchant a cuckold? You must say he is one of the livery. Is a great lord a fool? You must say he is weak. Is a gallant pocky? You must say he has the court scab. Come, she's your mistress, or so.

Enter FRANCESCHINA *with her lute*

– Come, siren, your voice!

FRANCESCHINA

Vill not you stay in mine bosom tonight, love?

FREEVILL

By no means, sweet breast; this gentleman has vowed to see me chastely laid.

89 *sometimes elected* formerly chosen one

91 *Curtian gulfs* The Roman soldier, Marcus Curtius, leapt fully armed and on horseback, into a chasm which had opened in the forum, by his sacrifice causing it to close again and thus saving the city.

95 *short-heels* wanton (the origin of the term being that on short heels one is easily tipped onto one's back)

95–6 *there . . . face* i.e. she would scratch my eyes out

97 *sometimes* former

98 *enforcive* compelling

100–1 *cockatrice* This fabulous animal was supposed to kill at a glance, as the glance of a whore could kill the soul.

102 *suppository* a whore is *supposita* (Lat. = placed underneath), and so comes to be associated with other things placed underneath, even though a suppository strictly speaking enters and is not entered. See 12.

104 *one . . . livery* i.e. one of the guild, in the club (of cuckolds). See 31n.

105 *pocky* afflicted with the pox

106–7 *your . . . so* i.e. let's say she's your mistress now. See I.i.107.

FRANCESCHINA
He shall have a bed, too, if dat it please him.

FREEVILL
Peace! you tender him offence. He is one of a professed abstinence. Siren, your voice, and away!

[FRANCESCHINA] (*She sings to her lute*)

The dark is my delight,
So 'tis the nightingale's.
My music's in the night,
So is the nightingale's.
My body is but little,
So is the nightingale's.
I love to sleep 'gainst prickle,
So doth the nightingale.

[FREEVILL]
Thanks. Buss! [*he and Franceschina kiss*] So. The night grows old; good rest.

FRANCESCHINA
Rest to mine dear love; rest, and no long absence.

FREEVILL
Believe me, not long.

FRANCESCHINA
Sall ick not believe you long? *Exit*

FREEVILL
O yes. [*to Page*] Come, *via*! Away, boy! On!

Exit, his Page lighting him

Enter FREEVILL *and seems to overhear* MALHEUREUX

MALHEUREUX
Is she unchaste? Can such a one be damned?
O love and beauty, ye two eldest seeds
Of the vast chaos, what strong right you have
Even in things divine, our very souls!

115 s.p. ed. (*not in* Q)

115–22 The setting for this song is to be found in BM Add. MS 24665 and is reproduced by Andrew J. Sabol, 'Two Unpublished Stage Songs for the "Aery of Children" ', *Renaissance News*, 13, Autumn 1960, pp. 222–32 (Wine).

121 The nightingale was traditionally depicted as sleeping with its breast against a thorn, symbolising the torments of love. The whore sleeps against the penis of her customer.

123 s.p. ed. (*not in* Q)
Buss Kiss (vigorously)

123 s.d. (*not in* Q)

127 i.e. shall I not trust you for long?

128 *via* away

FREEVILL

[*Aside*] Wa, ha, ho! Come, bird, come! Stand, peace!

MALHEUREUX

Are strumpets, then, such things so delicate?
Can custom spoil what nature made so good?
Or is their custom bad? Beauty's for use.
I never saw a sweet face vicious;
It might be proud, inconstant, wanton, nice,
But never tainted with unnatural vice.
Their worst is, their best art is love to win.
O that to love should be or shame or sin!

FREEVILL

[*Aside*] By the Lord, he's caught! Laughter eternal!

MALHEUREUX

Soul, I must love her! Destiny is weak
To my affection. A common love?
Blush not, faint breast!
That which is ever loved of most is best.
Let colder eld the strong'st objections move;
No love's without some lust, no life without some love.

FREEVILL

[*to Malheureux*] Nay, come on, good sir; what though the most odious spectacle the world can present be an immodest, vulgar woman, yet, sir, for my sake –

MALHEUREUX

Well, sir, for your sake I'll think better of them.

FREEVILL

Do, good sir, and pardon me that have brought you in.
You know the sight of vice augments the hate of sin.

MALHEUREUX

Ha! Will you go home, sir? 'Tis high bedtime.

FREEVILL

With all my heart, sir; only do not chide me.
I must confess –

MALHEUREUX A wanton lover you have been.

FREEVILL

'O that to love should be or shame or sin!'

135 *custom* social convention; the provision of sexual services

138 *nice* lascivious

140 *Their worst is* i.e. the worst that can be said of them is

141 *or . . . or* either . . . or

143–5 ed. (Soule . . . affection. / A . . . breast Q)

144 *To* Compared with

147 *eld* old age

MALHEUREUX
Say ye?
FREEVILL
'Let colder eld the strong'st objections move!'
MALHEUREUX
How's this?
FREEVILL
'No love's without some lust, no life without some love!'
Go your ways for an *apostata*! I believe my cast garment must be let out in the seams for you, when all is done!
Of all the fools that would all man out-thrust,
He that 'gainst nature would seem wise is worst.

Exeunt

Act II, Scene i

Enter FREEVILL, *Pages with torches, and Gentlemen with music*

FREEVILL
The morn is yet but young. Here, gentlemen,
This is my Beatrice' window, this the chamber
Of my betrothed dearest, whose chaste eyes,
Full of loved sweetness and clear cheerfulness,
Have gaged my soul to her in joyings,
Shredding away all those weak under-branches
Of base affections and unfruitful heats.

162 *No . . . love* ed. (No . . . lust, / No . . . loue Q)
163 *apostata* apostate, deserter of one's faith
cast cast off
164 *must . . . done* i.e. because the 'raiment' of lust must be more ample to go with Malheureux' greater desire
165–6 Malheureux beforehand tried to thrust out of doors every natural human sexual desire ('all man'); but whoever strives to assert some sort of wisdom against the very nature of man itself is the worst of fools, as evidenced here by Malheureux' desertion of his principles.

0 s.d. *music* musical instruments. The music that would also undoubtedly have filled the interval between the acts at the Blackfriars would have made possible a break here in the action defined by Freevill's exit at the end of Act I and the same character's entrance at the beginning of Act II.
5 *gaged* pledged
in joyings in rejoicing. Q reads 'in ioyings' and not 'inioyings' and it seems appropriate to the context here to make a distinction between 'enjoying' one's beloved and 'rejoycing' in her, even though the single word could also be interpreted 'her enjoyment'.

Here bestow your music to my voice. (*sings*)
[*Exeunt Gentlemen and Pages*]

Enter BEATRICE *above*

Always a virtuous name to my chaste love!

BEATRICE
Loved sir,
The honour of your wish return to you.
I cannot with a mistress' compliment,
Forced discourses, or nice art of wit
Give entertain to your dear wished presence;
But safely thus: what hearty gratefulness,
Unsullen silence, unaffected modesty,
And an unignorant shamefastness can express,
Receive as your protested due. Faith, my heart,
I am your servant.
O let not my secure simplicity
Breed your mislike, as one quite void of skill;
'Tis grace enough in us not to be ill.
I can some good, and, faith, I mean no hurt;
Do not, then, sweet, wrong sober ignorance.
I judge you all of virtue, and our vows
Should kill all fears that base distrust can move.
My soul, what say you? Still you love?

FREEVILL Still.
My vow is up above me and, like time,
Irrevocable. I am sworn all yours.
No beauty shall untwine our arms, no face
In my eyes can or shall seem fair;
And would to God only to me you might

8 s.d. 1 (*Cantat.* Q)
10–11 ed. (*as one line* Q)
13 *nice* sophisticated
14 *entertain* audience
17 *shamefastness* modesty
18 *your protested due* the due I protest is yours
20 *secure* trusting
20–1 1633 (O . . . mislike, / As . . . skill, Q)
21 *as* since I am
22 *ill* wicked
24 *sober* unaffectedly plain
25 *all of virtue* entirely virtuous
27 *Still.* ed. (Still? Q) i.e. Always.
27–8 *Still. / My . . . time,* ed. (*as one line* Q)

Seem only fair! Let others disesteem
Your matchless graces, so might I safer seem.
Envy I covet not: far, far be all ostent,
Vain boasts of beauties, soft joys, and the rest;
He that is wise pants on a private breast.
So could I live in desert most unknown;
Yourself to me enough were populous.
Your eyes shall be my joys, my wine that still
Shall drown my often cares. Your only voice
Shall cast a slumber on my list'ning sense.
You with soft lip shall only ope mine eyes
And suck their lids asunder. Only you
Shall make me wish to live, and not fear death,
So on your cheeks I might yield latest breath.
O he that thus may live and thus shall die
May well be envied of a deity!

BEATRICE
Dear my loved heart, be not so passionate;
Nothing extreme lives long.

FREEVILL
But not to be
Extreme – nothing in love's extreme! – my love
Receives no mean.

BEATRICE
I give you faith; and, prithee,
Since, poor soul, I am so easy to believe thee,
Make it much more pity to deceive me.
Wear this slight favour in my remembrance.

Throweth down a ring to him

FREEVILL
Which when I part from, hope, the best of life,
Ever part from me.

33 *only fair* the only fair one
35 *ostent* ostentation
40 *still* always
41 *often* frequent
Your only Only your
46 *So* Provided that
latest last
50–2 *But . . . mean* i.e. how can it be that I should not feel extreme in my passion? – is it then that there is no extremity in true love, as you say? let me try to believe this! – but my love is not just moderately aroused by you
50–4 *But . . . me* ed. (*as prose* Q)
56–7 ed. (Which . . . from, / hope . . . me. Q)

BEATRICE
I take you and your word, which may ever live your servant.
See, day is quite broke up – the best of hours.

FREEVILL
Good morrow, graceful mistress. Our nuptial day holds.

BEATRICE
With happy constancy, a wished day. *Exit*

FREEVILL
Myself and all content rest with you.

Enter MALHEUREUX

MALHEUREUX
The studious morn with paler cheek draws on
The day's bold light. Hark how the free-born birds
Carol their unaffected passions!

The nightingales sing

Now sing they sonnets; thus they cry, 'We love.'
O breath of heaven! Thus they, harmless souls,
Give entertain to mutual affects.
They have no bawds, no mercenary beds,
No politic restraints, no artificial heats,
No faint dissemblings; no custom makes them blush,
No shame afflicts their name. O you happy beasts,
In whom an inborn heat is not held sin,
How far transcend you wretched, wretched man,
Whom national custom, tyrannous respects
Of slavish order, fetters, lames his power,
Calling that sin in us which in all things else
Is nature's highest virtue!
O miseri quorum gaudia crimen habent!

58 *which ... servant* i.e. may your word ever be true to you (so that I can rely on it)
59 *broke up* i.e. has broken up the clouds of darkness
60 *holds* is securely fixed
61 *constancy* certainty
62 s.d. ed. (*after 61* Q)
63 *studious* The image is of the studious scholar, with the pallor of the library upon him, already at work as appropriately pale dawn breaks to bring in its wake the full sunlight of the day.
65 s.d. No doubt boys of the company in some way imitating the nightingale's song, singing thus (66) the nightingale's 'sonnets' (i.e. love songs).
68 i.e. express mutual affections
69 *mercenary* for hire
70 *politic* socially contrived 78–9 1633 (*as one line* Q)
79 'O they are wretched whose joys are judged criminal', quoted from Maximianus' *Pseudo-Gallus* (I.180) by Montaigne (III.v.129).

Sure nature against virtue cross doth fall,
Or virtue's self is oft unnatural.
That I should love a strumpet! I, a man of snow!
Now, shame forsake me, whither am I fallen!
A creature of a public use! My friend's love, too!
To live to be a talk to men, a shame
To my professed virtue! O accursed reason,
How many eyes hast thou to see thy shame,
And yet how blind once to prevent defame!

FREEVILL

Diaboli virtus in lumbis est. Morrow, my friend. Come, I could make a tedious scene of this now, but what, pah! – thou art in love with a courtesan? Why, sir, should we loathe all strumpets, some men should hate their own mothers or sisters; a sin against kind, I can tell you.

MALHEUREUX

May it beseem a wise man to be in love?

FREEVILL

Let wise men alone; 'twill beseem thee and me well enough.

MALHEUREUX

Shall I not offend the vow-band of our friendship?

FREEVILL

What, to affect that which thy friend affected? By heaven, I resign her freely. The creature and I must grow off. By this time she has assuredly heard of my resolved marriage, and no question swears, 'God's sacrament, ten tousand divels!' I'll resign, i'faith.

80 *cross* athwart

82 *man of snow* i.e. cold-blooded, not given to passion. See I.ii.79–80.

88 *defame* disgrace

89 *Diaboli . . . est* 'The strength of the devil is in our loins', quoted from St Jerome by Montaigne (III.v.102).

93 *kind* nature

94–6 Montaigne's drift at this point is in the opposite direction: 'A young man demanded of the Philosopher *Panetius*, whether it would beseeme a wise man to be in love; *Let wisemen alone* (quoth he) *but for thee and me that are not so, it were best not to engage our selves into so stirring and violent a humour, which makes us slaves to others and contemptible unto our selves*' (Montaigne III.v.146).

97 *vow-band* ed. (vowe band Q) i.e. sworn bond

98 *to . . . affected* i.e. to love the woman your friend also was drawn to love

99 *grow off* grow apart, separate

100 *assuredly* ed. (assurely Q)

101 *question* doubt

MALHEUREUX

I would but embrace her, hear her speak, and at the most but kiss her.

FREEVILL

O friend, he that could live with the smoke of roast meat might live at a cheap rate!

MALHEUREUX

I shall ne'er prove heartily received;
A kind of flat ungracious modesty,
An insufficient dullness, stains my 'haviour.

FREEVILL

No matter, sir. Insufficiency and sottishness are much commendable in a most discommendable action. Now could I swallow thee! Thou hadst wont to be so harsh and cold. I'll tell thee:
Hell and the prodigies of angry Jove
Are not so fearful to a thinking mind
As a man without affection. Why, friend,
Philosophy and nature are all one;
Love is the centre in which all lines close,
The common bond of being.

MALHEUREUX

O, but a chaste, reserved privateness,
A modest continence!

FREEVILL

I'll tell thee what, take this as firmest sense:
Incontinence will force a continence;
Heat wasteth heat, light defaceth light;
Nothing is spoiled but by his proper might.
This is something too weighty for thy floor.

105–6 *'He that could dine with the smoake of roste-meat, might he not dine at a cheape rate?'* (Montaigne III.v.130).

109 *insufficient dullness* inadequate lack of verve (with also a sexual connotation)

110–11 *Insufficiency . . . action 'Insufficiency and sottishnesse are commendable in a discommendable action'* (Montaigne III.v.145).

112 *swallow thee* i.e. be really at one with you

114–19 ed. (*as prose* Q)

118–19 '[love] is a matter everywhere infused; and a Centre whereto all lines come, all things looke' (Montaigne III.v.95–6).

120–1 ed. (*as one line* Q)

123 *'Belike we must be incontinent that we may be continent*, burning is quenched by fire' (Montaigne III.v.97).

125 *proper* own

126 i.e. my argument is too great a burden for you to bear

MALHEUREUX

But howsoe'er you shade it, the world's eye
Shines hot and open on't.
Lying, malice, envy are held but slidings,
Errors of rage, when custom and the world
Calls lust a crime spotted with blackest terrors.

FREEVILL

Where errors are held crimes, crimes are but errors. Along, sir, to her! She is an arrant strumpet; and a strumpet is a serpigo, venomed gonorrhoea to man – things actually possessed. Yet since thou art in love –

Offers to go out, and suddenly draws back

and again, as good make use of a statue, a body without a soul, a carcass three months dead – yet since thou art in love –

MALHEUREUX

Death, man, my destiny I cannot choose!

FREEVILL

Nay, I hope so – again, they sell but only flesh, no jot affection; so that even in the enjoying, *Absentem marmoreamque putes.* Yet since you needs must love –

MALHEUREUX

Unavoidable, though folly worse than madness!

127–8 i.e. just as the sun (which is in a literal sense the world's eye) eventually penetrates all shade, so however lust is disguised it is subject in the end to the world's condemnation

129 *slidings* slight faults

132 'we see that in places where faults are bewitchings, bewitchings are but faults' (Montaigne III.v.141)

132–8 *Along . . . love* 1633 (Along . . . strumpet is / A . . . man / Things . . . loue / And . . . Statue, / A . . . dead, / Yet . . . loue. Q)

134 *serpigo* skin disease, here associated with venereal infection

134–5 *things . . . possessed* i.e. the diseases of love are really owned by the sufferer, unlike the strumpet he loves

135 s.d. ed. (*after* man *in 134* Q)

140–2 ed. (Nay . . . flesh, / No . . . enioying, / *Absentem* . . . loue. Q)

141–2 *Absentem . . . putes* 'you would think her absent and made of marble', slightly misquoting Martial (*Epigrammata* XI.lx.8), correctly quoted as *marmoreamve* (= or made of marble) by Montaigne (III.v.133).

FREEVILL

It's true;
But since you needs must love, you must know this:
He that must love, a fool and he must kiss. –

Enter COCLEDEMOY

Master Cocledemoy, *ut vales, domine!*

COCLEDEMOY

Ago tibi gratias, my worshipful friend. How does your friend?

FREEVILL

Out, you rascal!

COCLEDEMOY

Hang toasts, you are an ass! Much o' your worship's brain lies in your calves. Bread o' God, boy, I was at supper last night with a new-weaned bulchin – bread o' God, drunk, horribly drunk, horribly drunk! There was a wench, one Frank Frailty, a punk, an honest polecat, of a clean instep, sound leg, smooth thigh, and the nimble devil in her buttock. Ah, fist o' grace! When saw you Tysefew or Master Caqueteur, that prattling gallant of a good draught, common customs, fortunate impudence, and sound fart?

FREEVILL

Away, rogue!

COCLEDEMOY

Hang toasts, my fine boy, my companions are worshipful!

MALHEUREUX

Yes, I hear you are taken up with scholars and churchmen.

Enter HOLIFERNES *the Barber['s boy]*

144–5 1633 (*as one line* Q)
146 *a . . . kiss* i.e. a fool and he are the same person
147 *ut . . . domine* good day, sir
148 *Ago . . . gratias* Thank you. See 163n.
153 *bulchin* bull-calf, i.e. gallant
155 *Frank Frailty* a play on Franceschina's name, 'Frank' rhyming with the first syllable, and 'Frailty' a usual name for a prostitute
punk whore
polecat whore
clean instep trim, pretty feet
157 *fist* fart
158 *prattling* translates Caqueteur's name
draught capacity for drinking at a single pull
158–9 *common customs* i.e. whoring

COCLEDEMOY

Quamquam te, Marce fili, my fine boy. [*to Freevill*] Does your worship want a barber-surgeon?

FREEVILL

Farewell, knave! Beware the Mulligrubs!

Exeunt FREEVILL *and* MALHEUREUX

COCLEDEMOY

Let the Mulligrubs beware the knave! – What, a barber-surgeon, my delicate boy?

HOLIFERNES

Yes, sir, an apprentice to surgery.

[COCLEDEMOY]

'Tis my fine boy. To what bawdy house doth your master belong? What's thy name?

HOLIFERNES

Holifernes Reinscure.

COCLEDEMOY

Reinscure? Good Master Holifernes, I desire your further acquaintance – nay, pray ye be covered, my fine boy; kill thy itch and heal thy scabs. Is thy master rotten?

163 *Quamquam ... fili* 'Although, Marcus my son ...', the opening words of Cicero's *De Officiis*, a prominent contributor to Cocledemoy's probably small stock of Latin (see I.ii.63n), which which he irritatingly holds his own against gentlemen (see 147–50). The only colour of justification for the fragment of Latin here is that Cocledemoy is also addressing a boy. See Introduction p. xvi and IV.iii.8n.

164 *barber-surgeon* The two functions went together at this time, the medical and the cosmetic. Cocledemoy impudently enquires whether Freevill is in need of the medical services.

167 *delicate* Still in Latin vein, Cocledemoy uses the word with *delicatus* in mind, which meant 'attractive, charming' (often in a sexual sense).

169 s.p. 1633 (*not in* Q)

171 The first name is of the great general of Nabuchodonosor, killed by Judith (Judith 13.8), but is here pleasing because of its largeness for a little boy and its touch of the infernal appropriately leading to the second name, which refers to the cure of the loins or kidneys of sufferers from the pox.

173 *be covered* put your hat back on (which he had removed as the usual mark of respect to a superior or an elder)

174 *itch ... scabs* symptoms of venereal disease
rotten either rotten with disease or in his grave

HOLIFERNES
My father, forsooth, is dead –

COCLEDEMOY
And laid in his grave.
Alas, what comfort shall Peggy then have?

HOLIFERNES
None but me, sir, that's my mother's son, I assure you.

COCLEDEMOY
Mother's son? A good witty boy; would live to read an homily well. And to whom are you going now?

HOLIFERNES
Marry, forsooth, to trim Master Mulligrub the vintner.

COCLEDEMOY
Do you know Master Mulligrub?

HOLIFERNES
My godfather, sir.

COCLEDEMOY
Good boy! Hold up thy chops. I pray thee do one thing for me. My name is Gudgeon.

HOLIFERNES
Good Master Gudgeon.

COCLEDEMOY
Lend me thy basin, razor, and apron. [*takes them*]

HOLIFERNES
O Lord, sir!

COCLEDEMOY
Well spoken; good English! But what's thy furniture worth?

HOLIFERNES
O Lord, sir, I know not.

COCLEDEMOY
Well spoken; a boy of good wit! Hold this pawn. Where dost dwell?

175 *forsooth* in truth

175–6 *And ... have?* 1633 (*as prose* Q)
Cocledemoy possibly repeating some words from a song. Bullen suggests that they are from 'A ballad intytuled *Peggies Complaint for the Death of her Willye*', which was entered in the Stationers' Register on 26 September 1588.

177 *that's* who is

178–9 *would ... well* i.e. would make a good clergyman, falling in so easily with the conventional moralising shape here

183 *chops* jaws, i.e. hold your head up boldly

184 *Gudgeon* a small fresh-water fish used for bait, appropriately

186 s.d. (*not in* Q)

188 *furniture* equipment

191 *pawn* pledge

HOLIFERNES

At the sign of the Three Razors, sir.

COCLEDEMOY

A sign of good shaving, my catastrophonical fine boy. I have an odd jest to trim Master Mulligrub for a wager. A jest, boy, a humour! I'll return thy things presently. Hold!

HOLIFERNES

What mean you, good Master Gudgeon?

COCLEDEMOY

Nothing, faith, but a jest, boy. Drink that. [*gives money*] I'll recoil presently.

HOLIFERNES

You'll not stay long?

COCLEDEMOY

As I am an honest man. The Three Razors?

HOLIFERNES

Ay, sir. *Exit*

COCLEDEMOY

Good! and if I shave not Master Mulligrub, my wit has no edge, and I may go cack in my pewter. Let me see – a barber. My scurvy tongue will discover me; must dissemble, must disguise. For my beard, my false hair; for my tongue – Spanish, Dutch, or Welsh? – no, a Northern barber! Very good. Widow Reinscure's man, well. Newly entertained, right. So. Hang toasts! All cards have white backs, and all knaves would seem to have white breasts. So, proceed now, worshipful Cocledemoy.

Exit COCLEDEMOY *in his barber's furniture*

194 *catastrophonical* A joke word, for which Wood suggests a meaning derived from 'catastrophe' (= jokingly used for 'buttocks') and the Greek *phoneo* (= to sound), which gives 'farting'.

195 *trim* shave, clip; cheat

196 *Hold* Wait a moment (presumably feeling for money to give the boy, who has already had a 'pawn' (an object of some sort) at 191)

199 *recoil* return

203 *shave* here has more the sense of 'fleece'

204 *cack . . . pewter* shit in my cup (or perhaps the pewter is the barber's basin he will be using)

208 *entertained* employed

209–10 *All . . . breasts* Playing cards were usually white, or plain, at the back to prevent their being easily marked, so the 'white breasts' of knaves are their proclamation of innocence. Walley suggests that Cocledemoy puts on a barber's white apron here.

[Act II, Scene ii]

Enter MARY FAUGH *and* FRANCESCHINA, *with her hair loose, chafing*

MARY FAUGH

Nay, good sweet daughter, do not swagger so. You hear your love is to be married, true; he does cast you off, right; he will leave you to the world – what then? Though blue and white, black and green leave you, may not red and yellow entertain you? Is there but one colour in the rainbow?

FRANCESCHINA

Grand grincome on your sentences! God's sacrament, ten tousand divels take you! You ha' brought mine love, mine honour, mine body, all to noting!

MARY FAUGH

To nothing? I'll be sworn I have brought them to all the things I could. I ha' made as much o' your maidenhead – and you had been mine own daughter, I could not ha' sold your maidenhead oft'ner than I ha' done. I ha' sworn for you, God forgive me! I have made you acquainted with the Spaniard, Don Skirtoll; with the Italian, Master Beieroane; with the Irish lord, Sir Patrick; with the Dutch merchant, Haunce Herkin Glukin Skellam Flapdragon; and specially with the greatest French; and now lastly with this English – yet in my conscience, an honest gentleman. And am I now grown one of the accursed with you for my labour? Is this my reward? Am I called bawd? Well, Mary Faugh, go thy ways, Mary Faugh; thy kind heart will bring thee to the hospital.

0 s.d. *chafing* storming angrily

1 *swagger* rage

6 *grincome* syphilis
sentences platitudinous remarks

14 *Skirtoll* From the wide slops, or knickerbockers, fashionable in Spain.

15 *Beieroane* This puzzling word may well be the result of a compositor's error: but Italians were thought to be fond of anal sex, and something like 'buy your an(us)' may be behind it.
Sir ed. (S. Q)

16 *Glukin Skellam* 'Glukin' may suggest a gurgling sound (the Dutch were notorious drinkers); 'Skellam' is from Dutch *Schelm* = rogue.

17 *greatest French* An allusion not only to nobility, but perhaps also to sexual size (?by contrast with 'Flapdragon' at 16 (but see also IV.i.56–7n), and to the 'great' or French pox.

22 *hospital* poor-house

FRANCESCHINA

Nay, good naunt, you'll help me to anoder love, vill you not?

MARY FAUGH

Out, thou naughty belly! Wouldst thou make me thy bawd? Thou'st best make me thy bawd; I ha' kept counsel for thee. Who paid the apothecary? Was't not honest Mary Faugh? Who redeemed thy petticoat and mantle? Was't not honest Mary Faugh? Who helped thee to thy custom, not of swaggering Ireland captains nor of two-shilling Inns o' Court men, but with honest flat-caps, wealthy flat-caps, that pay for their pleasure the best of any men in Europe, nay, which is more, in London? And dost thou defy me, vile creature?

FRANCESCHINA

Foutra 'pon you, vitch, bawd, polecat! Paugh! did you not praise Freevill to mine love?

MARY FAUGH

I did praise, I confess, I did praise him. I said he was a fool, an unthrift, a true whoremaster, I confess; a constant drab-keeper, I confess. But what, the wind is turned.

FRANCESCHINA

It is, it is, vile woman, reprobate woman, naughty woman, it is! Vat sall become of mine poor flesh now? Mine body

23 *naunt* bawd (affectionate variant of 'aunt')

26–7 *kept . . . thee* kept your secrets

30 *two-shilling* The fee for a whore's services to be expected from 'Inns o' Court men' (i.e. barristers or law students from one of the four main legal societies in London, the resort of privileged but not necessarily rich young men finishing their education; the four Inns were Lincoln's Inn, Inner Temple, Middle Temple, and Gray's Inn). 'A journeyman earned between about seven shillings and nine shillings a week at this time' (Davison).

31 *honest flat-caps* ed. (honest atte-cappes Q, *the fl ligature failing to print, most likely because it has fallen out of the forme at a loose margin*) i.e. citizens, tradesmen (so called from the flat woollen caps they wore)

35 *Foutra 'pon you* i.e. fuck off (Fr. *foutre* = to fuck)

36 *praise* i.e. commend

38 *unthrift* spendthrift

true . . . constant These two words are not only ordinarily intensive, but in the sense of keeping to one mistress.

38–9 *drab-keeper* haunter of whores

40 *reprobate* i.e. in Calvinist theology, one of the damned as distinct from one of the elect. Mary Faugh has been defined before this in relation to extreme Protestant notions. See I.ii.19–20n.

must turn Turk for twopence. O Divela, life o' mine art! Ick sall be revenged! Do ten tousand hell damn me, ick sall have the rogue troat cut; and his love, and his friend, and all his affinity sall smart, sall die, sall hang! Now legion of divel seize him! De gran' pest, St. Anthony's fire, and de hot Neapolitan poc rot him!

Enter FREEVILL *and* MALHEUREUX

FREEVILL
Franceschina!

FRANCESCHINA
O mine seet, dear'st, kindest, mine loving! O mine tousand, ten tousand, delicated, petty seetart! Ah, mine aderlievest affection! [*kisses Freevill*]

FREEVILL
Why, monkey, no fashion in you? Give entertain to my friend.

FRANCESCHINA
Ick sall make de most of you dat courtesy may. – Aunt Mary! Mettre Faugh! Stools, stools for dese gallants! (*Sings in the French style*)

42 *turn . . . twopence* i.e. engage in damnable practices (as a Turk, being an infidel, would be damned) for paltry gain; this may be a glance forward at the sort of whore's life she is now to lead, the rewards paltry by comparison with Freevill's love, or it may be a glance back at what that whore's life, which once promised Freevill, has come to.
art heart

43 *Do* Though (in Franceschina's accented speech)
tousand ed. (thousand Q, *emended on the assumption that the compositor mistakenly set a correct, non-foreign spelling for one of Franceschina's habitually accented pronunciations*)

45 *affinity* kindred

46 *divel* (deuill Q, *see textual note at 43*)
pest plague
St. Anthony's fire Erysipelas (feverish skin disease)

49 *seet* sweet

50 *delicated* delicate. See II.i.167n.

51 *aderlievest* ed. (a deere leeuest Q)

51 s.d. (*not in* Q)

52–3 *no . . . friend* i.e. kiss Malheureux as she has just kissed Freevill. There was a fashion for kissing ladies quite freely as a form of greeting. See I.ii.86 and III.i.10–24.

55 *Mettre* Mistress

55 s.d. (*Cantat Gallice.* Q, *printed centred after* seetart! *in 50*) *in the French style* i.e. briskly

Mine mettre sing non oder song –
  Frolic, frolic, sir –
But still complain me do her wrong –
  Lighten your heart, sir.
For me did but kiss her,
For me did but kiss her,
  And so let go.

[*to Freevill*] Your friend is very heavy. Ick sall ne'er like such sad company.

FREEVILL

No, thou delightest only in light company.

FRANCESCHINA

By mine trot, he been very sad. – Vat ail you, sir?

MALHEUREUX

A toothache, lady, a paltry rheum.

FRANCESCHINA

De diet is very goot for de rheum.

FREEVILL

How far off dwells the house-surgeon, Mary Faugh?

MARY FAUGH

You are a profane fellow, i'faith. I little thought to hear such ungodly terms come from your lips.

FRANCESCHINA [*seeing and grasping a ring on Freevill's finger*]

Pridee now, 'tis but a toy, a very trifle.

FREEVILL

I care not for the value, Frank, but i'faith –

FRANCESCHINA

I'fait, me must needs have it. [*Aside*] Dis is Beatrice' ring.

56–62 ed. (*as prose* Q)
'a version of lute song XIX from Robert Jones, *First Book of Songs and Airs* (1600); an anonymous setting from a British Library manuscript is reproduced by Andrew J. Sabol, *Renaissance News*, 13 (1960), 222–32' (Jackson and Neill). The apparently prose asides at 57 and 59 I imagine attracted into the song.

64 *sad* sober, grave

65 *light* merry; wanton

66 *trot* troth, i.e. faith

67 *rheum* cold

68 *diet* See I.ii.25n.

69 *house-surgeon* Freevill implies that Mary Faugh's 'house' is so fertile a producer of disease that it needs its own doctor.

72 s.d. (*not in* Q)
toy thing of no value, trinket. The wordless stage business that must precede this sudden line, as the ring glitters in Franceschina's grasp of Freevill's hand, must be rather as happened at I.i.47.

O could I get it! [*to Freevill*] Seet, pridee now, as ever you have embraced me with a hearty arm, a warm thought, or a pleasing touch, as ever you will profess to love me, as ever you do wish me life, give me dis ring, dis little ring.

FREEVILL

Prithee be not uncivilly importunate; sha' not ha't. Faith, I care not for thee nor thy jealousy. Sha' not ha'it, i'faith.

FRANCESCHINA

You do not love me. I hear of Sir Hubert Subboys' daughter, Mistress Beatrice. God's sacrament, ick could scratch out her eyes and suck the holes!

FREEVILL

Go, y'are grown a punk rampant!

FRANCESCHINA

So! Get thee gone! Ne'er more behold min eyes, by thee made wretched!

FREEVILL

Mary Faugh, farewell. – Farewell, Frank.

[*Exit* MARY FAUGH]

FRANCESCHINA

Sall I not ha' de ring?

FREEVILL

No, by the Lord!

FRANCESCHINA

By te Lord?

FREEVILL

By the Lord!

FRANCESCHINA

Go to your new blowze, your unproved sluttery, your modest mettre, forsooth!

FREEVILL

Marry, will I, forsooth!

FRANCESCHINA

Will you marry, forsooth?

84 *rampant* violent, arrant (with an allusion to the heraldic use of the term)

87 Mary Faugh takes the hint and leaves, but Franceschina is not so easily got rid of.

90 Franceschina repeats scornfully Freevill's high-toned oath, which he then reaffirms, asserting the high tone of his new love for Beatrice.

92 *blowze* beggar's wench
unproved 1633 (vnproude Q). 1633 reads 'unprou'd', and gives the reading here (= virgin, untried), so that 'unproved' goes with 'sluttery' (= slut) as 'new' does with 'blowze'; but it would be possible to read Q's 'vnproude' as 'unproud' (= not fastidious) to chime evidently with the idea of a slut.

FREEVILL

Do not turn witch before thy time. [*to Malheureux*] With all my heart, sir, you will stay.

MALHEUREUX

I am no whit myself. *Video meliora proboque,*
But raging lust my fate all strong doth move:
The gods themselves cannot be wise and love.

FREEVILL

Your wishes to you. *Exit*

MALHEUREUX

Beauty entirely choice –

FRANCESCHINA

Pray ye, prove a man of fashion and neglect the neglected.

MALHEUREUX

Can such a rarity be neglected? Can there be measure or sin in loving such a creature?

FRANCESCHINA

O min poor forsaken heart!

MALHEUREUX

I cannot contain; he saw thee not that left thee.
If there be wisdom, reason, honour, grace
Or any foolishly esteemed virtue
In giving o'er possession of such beauty,
Let me be vicious, so I may be loved.
Passion, I am thy slave! Sweet, it shall be my grace
That I account thy love my only virtue.
Shall I swear I am thy most vowed servant?

FRANCESCHINA

Mine vowed? Go, go, go! I can no more of love. No, no, no! You bin all unconstant. O unfaithful men, tyrants, betrayers! De very enjoying us loseth us; and, when you only ha' made us hateful, you only hate us. O mine forsaken heart!

96–7 ed. (Doe ... time. / With ... stay. Q)

98 *no whit* not at all

Video ... proboque 'I see what is better and I approve it' (Ovid, *Metamorphoses* VII. 20); the text continues: *deteriora sequor* (= 'I follow what is worse'). In Ovid this is Medea struggling with her passion for Jason.

104 *rarity* rare excellence *measure* moderation, restraint

107 *contain* i.e. keep to myself what I would express

109 *Or* 1633 (Of Q)

116–18 *O ... hate us* 'After they [women] have wholy yeelded themselves to the mercy of our faith and constancy, they have hazarded something: They are rare and difficult vertues: so soone as they are ours, we are no longer theirs' (Montaigne III.v.131).

MALHEUREUX
[*Aside*] I must not rave. Silence and modesty, two customary virtues. [*to Franceschina*] Will you be my mistress?

FRANCESCHINA
Mettres? Ha, ha, ha!

MALHEUREUX
Will you lie with me?

FRANCESCHINA
Lie with you? O, no! You men will out-lie any woman. Fait, me no more can love.

MALHEUREUX
No matter; let me enjoy your bed.

FRANCESCHINA
O vile man, vat do you tink on me? Do you take me to be a beast, a creature that for sense only will entertain love, and not only for love, love? O brutish abomination!

MALHEUREUX
Why, then, I pray thee love, and with thy love enjoy me.

FRANCESCHINA
Give me reason to affect you. Will you swear you love me?

MALHEUREUX
So seriously, that I protest no office so dangerous, no deed so unreasonable, no cost so heavy, but I vow to the utmost tentation of my best being to effect it.

FRANCESCHINA
Sall I, or can I, trust again? O fool,
How natural 'tis for us to be abused!
Sall ick be sure that no satiety,
No enjoying, not time, shall languish your affection?

MALHEUREUX
If there be aught in brain, heart, or hand
Can make you doubtless, I am your vowed servant.

FRANCESCHINA
Will you do one ting for me?

MALHEUREUX
Can I do it?

FRANCESCHINA
Yes, yes; but ick do not love dis same Freevill.

MALHEUREUX
Well?

120–1 *Silence . . . virtues* 'Silence and modestie are qualities verie convenient to civil conversation' (Montaigne I.xxv.183).

124 *out-lie* taking Malheureux' 'lie' not in the sense 'copulate' but in the sense 'deceive'

134 *tentation* exertion

FRANCESCHINA
Nay, I do hate him.

MALHEUREUX
So?

FRANCESCHINA
By this kiss, I hate him!

MALHEUREUX
I love to feel such oaths; swear again.

FRANCESCHINA
No, no. Did you ever hear of any that loved at the first sight?

MALHEUREUX
A thing most proper.

FRANCESCHINA
Now, fait, I judge it all incredible until this hour I saw you, pretty fair-eyed yout. Would you enjoy me?

MALHEUREUX
Rather than my breath; even as my being.

FRANCESCHINA
Vell, had ick not made a vow –

MALHEUREUX
What vow?

FRANCESCHINA
O let me forget it; it makes us both despair.

MALHEUREUX
Dear soul, what vow?

FRANCESCHINA
Ha! good morrow, gentle sir; endeavour to forget me, as I must be enforced to forget all men. Sweet mind rest in you!

MALHEUREUX
Stay, let not my desire burst me. O, my impatient heat endures no resistance, no protraction! There is no being for me but your sudden enjoying.

FRANCESCHINA
I do not love Freevill.

148 *swear* i.e. kiss

153 *yout* youth

160–1 *Sweet . . . you* i.e. keep to your innocence of spirit

164 *your . . . enjoying* immediately enjoying you

165–70 Marston must have had in mind a similar episode between Beatrice and Benedick in *Much Ado about Nothing* (IV.i.287); indeed he may have derived the name of his chaste heroine from this play, though somewhat inappropriately, since Shakespeare's heroine is more of a Crispinella.

MALHEUREUX
But what vow? what vow?
FRANCESCHINA
So long as Freevill lives, I must not love.
MALHEUREUX
Then he –
FRANCESCHINA
Must –
MALHEUREUX
Die!
FRANCESCHINA
Ay! – no –
There is no such vehemence in your affects;
Would I were anything, so he were not!
MALHEUREUX
Will you be mine when he is not?
FRANCESCHINA
Will I? Dear, dear breast, by this most zealous kiss – but I will not persuade you – but if you hate him that I loathe most deadly – yet as you please, I'll persuade noting.
MALHEUREUX
Will you be only mine?
FRANCESCHINA
Vill I? How hard 'tis for true love to dissemble! I am only yours.
MALHEUREUX
'Tis as irrevocable as breath: he dies! –
Your love?
FRANCESCHINA – My vow! not until he be dead;
Which that I may be sure not to infringe,
Dis token of his death sall satisfy.
He has a ring, as dear as the air to him,
His new love's gift: tat got and brought to me,
I shall assured your professed rest.
MALHEUREUX
To kill a man?
FRANCESCHINA
O, done safely; a quarrel sudden picked, with an advan-

171–2 (*as one line* Q)
172 *affects* disposition
181–2 ed. (*as one line* Q)
182 i.e. now will you love me?
187 i.e. assuredly remain promised to you
professed 1633 (pofessed Q)

tage strike; then bribe – a little coin, all's safe, dear soul.
But I'll not set you on.

MALHEUREUX

Nay, he is gone. The ring. – Well come, little more liberal
of thy love.

FRANCESCHINA

Not yet – my vow –

MALHEUREUX O heaven, there is no hell
But love's prolongings! Dear, farewell.

FRANCESCHINA Farewell.
[*Aside*] Now does my heart swell high, for my revenge
Has birth and form. First, friend sall kill his friend;
He dat survives, I'll hang; besides, de chaste
Beatrice I'll vex. Only de ring –
Dat got, the world sall know the worst of evils:
Woman corrupted is the worst of devils. *Exit*

MALHEUREUX

To kill my friend! O 'tis to kill myself!
Yet man's but man's excrement, man breeding man
As he does worms, or this. (*He spits*) To spoil this, nothing!
The body of a man is of the selfsame soil
As ox or horse; no murder to kill these.
As for that only part which makes us man,
Murder wants power to touch't. – O wit, how vile,
How hellish art thou when thou raisest nature
'Gainst sacred faith! Think more – to kill a friend
To gain a woman, to lose a virtuous self
For appetite and sensual end, whose very having
Loseth all appetite and gives satiety,
That corporal end remorse and inward blushings,
Forcing us loathe the steam of our own heats,

194–5 ed. (*as prose* Q)

198 *hang* i.e. cause to be hanged

198–9 *de chaste / Beatrice* 1633 (de / Chast *Beatrice* Q)

201 proverbial (Tilley W641.648)

203–4 '*Aristippus*, who being urged with the affection he ought [i.e. owed] his children, as proceeding from his loynes, began to spit, saying, *That also that excrement proceeded from him, and that also we engendred wormes and lice*' (Montaigne I.xxvii.229).

204 s.d. ed. (*after* nothing! Q)
nothing Perhaps rubbing the spittle into the ground with his foot.

205 *soil* ed. (soule Q)

208 *wit* mind, intelligence

210–19 Montaigne contrasts 'lustful love' and friendship in rather similar terms (I.xxvii.231).

214 *remorse* i.e. gives remorse

Whilst friendship closed in virtue, being spiritual,
Tastes no such languishings and moment's pleasure
With much repentance, but like rivers flow,
And further that they run, they bigger grow.
Lord, how was I misgone! How easy 'tis to err
When passion will not give us leave to think!
A learn'd that is an honest man may fear,
And lust, and rage, and malice, and anything
When he is taken uncollected suddenly:
'Tis sin of cold blood, mischief with waked eyes,
That is the damned and the truly vice,
Not he that's passionless, but he 'bove passion's wise.
My friend shall know it all. *Exit*

[Act II, Scene iii]

Enter MASTER MULLIGRUB *and* MISTRESS MULLIGRUB, *she with* [*a*] *bag of money*

MISTRESS MULLIGRUB
It is right, I assure you, just fifteen pounds.

MULLIGRUB
Well, Cocledemoy, 'tis thou puttest me to this charge; but, and I catch thee, I'll charge thee with as many irons! Well, is the barber come? I'll be trimmed, and then to Cheapside to buy a fair piece of plate to furnish the loss. Is the barber come?

MISTRESS MULLIGRUB
Truth, husband, surely heaven is not pleased with our vocation. We do wink at the sins of our people, our wines are

216 *closed* joined together
220 *misgone* gone astray
223 *And lust* Both lust (the preceding comma needed to give this sense)
224 *uncollected* off guard
227 i.e. the wise man is not he who is without passion but he who is above it, masters it

0 s.d.2 *a bag* Q(u) (*bag* Q(c), *the omission in the corrected Bodleian* Q *here is clearly not a correction but an accidental dropping of a letter at a loose margin*)
4 *Cheapside* Market district of London
5 *furnish* make good (the loss of the goblets lamented at the beginning of the play)
8 *wink . . . people* i.e. drunkenness and fornication. See I.i.20–4.
8–9 *wines . . . Protestants* i.e. adulterated, not the 'true religion' (which for the Mulligrubs is their own belief – see I.i.146–7n – and not something they would class as sectarian – see IV.v.12; of course for them the allegedly protestant Church of England would in fact be adulterated with Popery). With a similar sense that Mulligrub's wines are 'heretical', Cocledemoy charges them at V.iii.107 with being 'Popish'.

Protestants, and – I speak it to my grief and to the burden of my conscience – we fry our fish with salt butter.

MULLIGRUB

Go, look to your business; mend the matter, and score false with a vengeance.

Exit [MISTRESS MULLIGRUB]

Enter COCLEDEMOY *like a barber*

Welcome, friend! Whose man?

COCLEDEMOY

Widow Reinscure's man, and shall please your good worship; my name's Andrew Shark.

MULLIGRUB

How does my godson, good Andrew?

COCLEDEMOY

Very well. He's gone to trim Master Quicquid, our parson. Hold up your head.

MULLIGRUB

How long have you been a barber, Andrew?

COCLEDEMOY

Not long, sir; this two year.

MULLIGRUB

What, and a good workman already? I dare scarce trust my head to thee.

COCLEDEMOY

O, fear not; we ha' polled better men than you. We learn the trade very quickly. Will your good worship be shaven or cut?

MULLIGRUB

As you will. What trade didst live by before thou turnedst barber, Andrew?

10 *salt butter* To complete this confession of the 'sins of the cellar' (I.i.43), Mistress Mulligrub laments the use of cheap Dutch (i.e. salted) butter instead of the good English sort. The salt put in to preserve the butter would also presumably stimulate the thirst of the customers.

11–12 *mend . . . vengeance* i.e. make up our loss by energetically overcharging those buying drinks on credit

12 s.d. 1 ed. (*after 10* Q)

15 *Andrew Shark* A shark to catch a shark (I.i.1). Cocledemoy's 'Northern barber' (II.i.207) is a cheating Scot, a sharking 'Andrew'.

17 *Quicquid* Whoever

18 *Hold . . . head* The echo of I.i.2–3 follows from 15.

23 *polled* i.e. trimmed; but the barbering terms, here and later in this episode, can easily take on knavish senses, so here 'gulled, plundered'. Mulligrub consistently misses Cocledemoy's innuendo, which of course the audience understands.

COCLEDEMOY

I was a pedlar in Germany, but my countrymen thrive better by this trade.

MULLIGRUB

What's the news, barber? Thou art sometimes at court?

COCLEDEMOY

Sometimes poll a page or so, sir.

MULLIGRUB

And what's the news? How do all my good lords and all my good ladies, and all the rest of my acquaintance?

COCLEDEMOY

[*Aside*] What an arrogant knave's this! I'll acquaintance ye! (*He spieth the bag*) 'Tis cash! [*to Mulligrub*] Say ye, sir?

MULLIGRUB

And what news? what news, good Andrew?

COCLEDEMOY

Marry, sir, you know the conduit at Greenwich and the under-holes that spouts up water?

MULLIGRUB

Very well; I was washed there one day, and so was my wife – you might have wrung her smock, i'faith. But what o' those holes?

COCLEDEMOY

Thus, sir: out of those little holes, in the midst of the night, crawled out twenty-four huge, horrible, monstrous, fearful, devouring –

MULLIGRUB

Bless us!

COCLEDEMOY

Serpents, which no sooner were beheld but they turned to mastiffs, which howled; those mastiffs instantly turned to cocks, which crowed; those cocks in a moment were changed to bears, which roared; which bears are at this

30 *sometimes . . . court* The court would have been full of Scotsmen since the accession of James I in 1603, all come for the pickings (28–9) in this satiric account; that 'Andrew' has been a barber 'this two year' (20) dates the play internally at 1605. See Introduction, p. xiii on Marston's fondness for dangerous anti-Scottish satire.

31 *poll* Here with a sexual innuendo (from the slang sense of 'pole') i.e. fuck. Both King James and his court were much suspected of homosexuality.

35 s.d. *He . . . bag* ed. (*after* Say ye, sir? *in 35* Q)

35 *Say ye* What was that you said?

37 *Greenwich* Downriver from London a little, a pleasurable place of resort for Londoners on a day's outing

39 *washed* soaked

hour to be yet seen in Paris Garden, living upon nothing but toasted cheese and green onions.

MULLIGRUB

By the Lord, and this may be! My wife and I will go see them; this portends something.

COCLEDEMOY

[*Aside*] Yes, worshipful fist, thou'st feel what portends by and by.

MULLIGRUB

And what more news? You shave the world, especially you barber-surgeons; you know the ground of many things; you are cunning privy searchers. By the mass, you scour all! What more news?

COCLEDEMOY

They say, sir, that twenty-five couple of Spanish jennets are to be seen hand in hand dance the old measures, whilst six goodly Flanders mares play to them on a noise of flutes.

MULLIGRUB

O monstrous! This is a lie, o' my word! Nay, and this be not a lie – I am no fool, I warrant! – nay, make an ass of me once –

COCLEDEMOY

Shut your eyes close; wink! Sure, sir, this ball will make you smart.

MULLIGRUB

I do wink.

COCLEDEMOY

Your head will take cold. I will put on your good worship's nightcap whilst I shave you.

COCLEDEMOY *puts on a coxcomb on* MULLIGRUB*'s head*

50 *Paris Garden* Bear-baiting arena on the south bank of the Thames
54 *fist* See II.i.157n.
57 *ground of* reasons behind
58 *privy searchers* priers into secret things, especially perhaps because of the intimate diagnosis of disease
scour attend minutely to
60 *jennets* small light horses of Spanish origin
61 *the old measures* the traditional stately dancing
62 *noise* consort
67 *wink* shut your eyes
ball ball of soap
71 s.d. ed. (*after* take cold. *in 70* Q);. *coxcomb* fool's cap

[*Aside*] So, mum! Hang toasts! Faugh! *Via!* Sparrows must peck and Cocledemoy munch.

[*Exit* COCLEDEMOY *with the bag*]

MULLIGRUB

Ha, ha, ha! Twenty-five couple of Spanish jennets to dance the old measures! Andrew makes my worship laugh, i'faith. Dost take me for an ass, Andrew? Dost know one Cocledemoy in town? He made me an ass last night, but I'll ass him! Art thou free, Andrew? Shave me well; I shall be one of the Common Council shortly; and, then, Andrew – why Andrew, Andrew, dost leave me in the suds? Why, Andrew, I shall be blind with winking. [*shouts*] Ha Andrew! Wife! Andrew! What means this? Wife! My money! Wife!

Enter MISTRESS MULLIGRUB

MISTRESS MULLIGRUB

What's the noise with you? What ail you?

MULLIGRUB

Where's the barber?

MISTRESS MULLIGRUB

Gone. I saw him depart long since. Why, are not you trimmed?

MULLIGRUB

Trimmed? O, wife, I am shaved! Did you take hence the money?

MISTRESS MULLIGRUB

I touched it not, as I am religious.

MULLIGRUB

O Lord, I have winked fair!

Enter HOLIFERNES

HOLIFERNES

I pray, godfather, give me your blessing.

MULLIGRUB

O Holifernes! O, where's thy mother's Andrew?

72 *mum* quiet
Via Exit

73 s.d. *with the bag* (*not in* Q)

78 *free* witty, saucy

79 *one . . . Council* i.e. an alderman of the city of London

81 s.d. (Cantat. *before* Why *in 81* Q). I suppose that Q's 'Cantat.' is an error for 'Clamat', since Mulligrub would hardly sing here.

90 *as . . . religious* i.e. on my conscience

HOLIFERNES

Blessing, godfather!

MULLIGRUB

The devil choke thee! Where's Andrew, thy mother's man?

HOLIFERNES

My mother hath none such, forsooth.

MULLIGRUB

My money – fifteen pounds! Plague of all Andrews! Who was't trimmed me?

HOLIFERNES

I know not, godfather; only one met me as I was coming to you, and borrowed my furniture, as he said, for a jest sake.

MULLIGRUB

What kind of fellow?

HOLIFERNES

A thick, elderly, stub-bearded fellow.

MULLIGRUB

Cocledemoy, Cocledemoy! Raise all the wise men in the street! I'll hang him with mine own hands! O wife, some *rosa solis*!

MISTRESS MULLIGRUB

Good husband, take comfort in the Lord. I'll play the devil, but I'll recover it. Have a good conscience; 'tis but a week's cutting in the term.

MULLIGRUB

O wife, O wife! O Jack! how does thy mother? – Is there any fiddlers in the house?

MISTRESS MULLIGRUB

Yes, Master Creak's noise.

MULLIGRUB

Bid 'em play, laugh, make merry. Cast up my accounts, for I'll go hang myself presently. I will not curse, but a pox

103 *thick* thick-set

104 *wise men* Mulligrub refers to his alert and capable neighbours here, without the more magical sense of the reference at the beginning of the play. See I.i.9n.

106 *rosa solis* 'a cordial or liqueur originally made from . . . the plant sundew, but subsequently composed of spirits (esp. brandy) with various essences or spices, sugar, etc.' (OED)

109 *week's . . . term* i.e. a week during term time of making customers pay for more than they get (the Inns of Court kept 'terms' that resemble our modern academic terms)

112 'Master Creak's noise' (i.e. consort) would go on to play the entr'acte music. Note how music is referred to at each of the act divisions in the play.

on Cocledemoy! He has polled and shaved me; he has trimmed me!

Exeunt

Act III, Scene i

Enter BEATRICE, CRISPINELLA, *and* NURSE PUTIFER

PUTIFER

Nay, good child, o' love, once more Master Freevill's sonnet o' the kiss you gave him!

BEATRICE

Sh'a't, good nurse. [*reads*]

Purest lips, soft banks of blisses,
Self alone deserving kisses,
O, give me leave to, etc.

CRISPINELLA

Pish, sister Beatrice! prithee read no more; my stomach o' late stands against kissing extremely.

BEATRICE

Why, good Crispinella?

CRISPINELLA

By the faith and trust I bear to my face, 'tis grown one of the most unsavoury ceremonies. Body o' beauty! 'tis one of the most unpleasing, injurious customs to ladies. Any fellow that has but one nose on his face, and standing collar and skirts also lined with taffety sarcenet, must salute us on the lips as familiarly – Soft skins save us! There was a stub-bearded John-a-Stile with a ployden's face saluted me last day and struck his bristles through my lips. I ha' spent ten shillings in pomatum since to skin them again!

1 *o' love* for love's sake

2 *sonnet* short love poem

3 *Sh'a't* (Thou) shalt have it

5 *Self* i.e. Themselves

10–24 'It is an unpleasing and injurious custome unto Ladies, that they must afford their lips to any man that hath but three Lackies following him, how unhandsome and lothsome soever he be' (Montaigne III.v.132).

13–14 *standing collar* fashionable high, starched collar

14 *skirts* lower part of gown or coat
taffety sarcenet fine silk

16 *John-a-Stile* fictitious name for a party to an action in a legal exemplum, like 'John Citizen'
ployden i.e. lawyer (from a variant of the name of Edmund Plowden (1518–85), a famous lawyer)

18 *pomatum* pomade
skin i.e. heal the chafed skin

Marry, if a nobleman or a knight with one lock visit us, though his unclean goose-turd-green teeth ha' the palsy, his nostrils smell worse than a putrefied marrowbone, and his loose beard drops into our bosom, yet we must kiss him with a cur'sy. A curse! For my part, I had as lief they would break wind in my lips.

BEATRICE

Fie, Crispinella! you speak too broad.

CRISPINELLA

No jot, sister. Let's ne'er be ashamed to speak what we be not ashamed to think. I dare as boldly speak venery as think venery.

BEATRICE

Faith, sister, I'll be gone if you speak so broad.

CRISPINELLA

Will you so? Now bashfulness seize you! We pronounce boldly robbery, murder, treason, which deeds must needs be far more loathsome than an act which is so natural, just, and necessary as that of procreation. You shall have an hypocritical vestal virgin speak that with close teeth publicly which she will receive with open mouth privately. For my own part, I consider nature without apparel; without disguising of custom or compliment, I give thoughts words, and words truth, and truth boldness. She whose honest freeness makes it her virtue to speak what she thinks, will make it her necessity to think what is good. I love no prohibited things, and yet I would have nothing prohibited by policy, but by virtue; for, as in the fashion of

20 *turd* 1633 (turnd Q)
goose-turd-green i.e. yellowish green

23 *cur'sy* curtsy, courtesy

26 *No jot* Not in the least

26–7 *Let's . . . think* '*Non pudeat dicere, quod non pudeat sentire. Let us not bee ashamed to speake, what we shame not to thinke*' (Montaigne III.v.77).

27 *venery* sex

30–5 *We . . . privately* 'Why was the acte of generation made so naturall, so necessary and so just, seeing we feare to speake of it without shame, and exclude it from our serious and regular discourses? we prononce boldly, to rob, to murther, to betray; and this we dare not but betweene our teeth' (Montaigne III.v.81).

35–40 *For . . . good* 'For my part I am resolved to dare speake whatsoever I dare do: And am displeased with thoughts not to be published. The worst of my actions or condicions seeme not so ugly unto me, as I finde it both ugly and base not to dare to avouch them . . . He that should be bound to tell all, should also bind himselfe to do nothing which one is forced to conceale' (Montaigne III.v.78).

40–5 *I . . . desired* 'Is it not herein as in matters of books, which being once called-in and forbidden become more saleable and publik' (Montaigne III.v.81).

time, those books that are called in are most in sale and request, so in nature those actions that are most prohibited are most desired.

BEATRICE

Good quick sister, stay your pace. We are private, but the world would censure you; for truly, severe modesty is women's virtue.

CRISPINELLA

Fie, fie! Virtue is a free, pleasant, buxom quality. I love a constant countenance well; but this froward, ignorant coyness, sour, austere, lumpish, uncivil privateness, that promises nothing but rough skins and hard stools – ha! fie o't! good for nothing but for nothing. – Well, nurse, and what do you conceive of all this?

PUTIFER

Nay, faith, my conceiving days be done. Marry, for kissing, I'll defend that; that's within my compass. But for my own part, here's Mistress Beatrice is to be married, with the grace of God. A fine gentleman he is shall have her, and I warrant a strong; he has a leg like a post, a nose like a lion, a brow like a bull, and a beard of most fair expectation. This week you must marry him, and I now will read a lecture to you both, how you shall behave yourselves to your husbands the first month of your nuptial. I ha' broke my skull about it, I can tell you, and there is much brain in it.

CRISPINELLA

Read it to my sister, good nurse, for I assure you I'll ne'er marry.

PUTIFER

Marry, God forfend! what will you do then?

CRISPINELLA

Faith, strive against the flesh. Marry? No, faith; husbands are like lots in the lottery: you may draw forty blanks before you find one that has any prize in him. A husband generally is a careless, domineering thing that grows like

43 *called in* withdrawn from circulation, forbidden

49–53 *Virtue ... nothing* 'I love a lightsome and civil discretion, and loathe a roughnes and austerity of behaviour: suspecting every peevish and wayward countenance ... *Vertue is a pleasant and human quality*' (Montaigne III.v.77).

49 *buxom* comely

56 *within my compass* i.e. I can still be kissed though I am past conceiving

60–1 *expectation* promise

63–4 *broke my skull* racked my brains

68 *forfend* forbid

coral, which as long as it is under water is soft and tender, but as soon as it has got his branch above the waves is presently hard, stiff, not to be bowed but burst; so when your husband is a suitor and under your choice, Lord, how supple he is, how obsequious, how at your service, sweet lady! Once married, got up his head above, a stiff, crooked, knobby, inflexible, tyrannous creature he grows; then they turn like water: more you would embrace, the less you hold. I'll live my own woman, and if the worst come to the worst, I had rather prove a wag than a fool.

BEATRICE

O, but a virtuous marriage –

CRISPINELLA

Virtuous marriage! There is no more affinity betwixt virtue and marriage than betwixt a man and his horse. Indeed, virtue gets up upon marriage sometimes and manageth it in the right way, but marriage is of another piece; for as a horse may be without a man, and a man without a horse, so marriage, you know, is often without virtue, and virtue, I am sure, more oft without marriage. But thy match, sister – by my troth, I think 'twill do well. He's a well-shaped, clean-lipped gentleman, of a handsome but not affected fineness, a good faithful eye, and a well-humoured cheek. Would he did not stoop in the shoulders, for thy sake! See, here he is.

Enter FREEVILL *and* TYSEFEW

73–9 The references to hardness and stiffness are a clear sexual innuendo behind the description of a husband's domineering temperament.

74 *his* its

75 *bowed but burst* bent but broken

80–1 *they . . . hold* 'it would be even, as if one should go about to graspe the water; for, how much the more he shal close and presse that, which by its owne nature is ever gliding, so much the more he shall loose what he would hold and fasten' (Montaigne II.xii.399–400).

82 *wag* a witty, merry person

84–90 'Those who thinke to honour marriage, by joyning love unto it, (in mine opinion) doe as those, who to doe vertue a favour, holde, that nobilitie is no other thing than Vertue. Indeed these things have affinitie; but therewithall great difference: their names and titles should not thus be commixt: both are wronged so to be confounded' (Montaigne III.v.85).

86 *manageth* i.e. as a horse is 'managed' when it is broken in or trained (the image of mounting a horse has a clear sexual connotation as well)

92 *clean-lipped* i.e. by contrast with 17

93 *fineness* fine appearance

well-humoured i.e. the four humours well proportioned, so as to produce a happy disposition

FREEVILL
Good day, sweet.

CRISPINELLA
Good morrow, brother. Nay, you shall have my lip. – Good morrow, servant.

TYSEFEW
Good morrow, sweet life.

CRISPINELLA
Life? Dost call thy mistress life?

TYSEFEW
Life, yes, why not life?

CRISPINELLA
How many mistresses hast thou?

TYSEFEW
Some nine.

CRISPINELLA
Why, then, thou hast nine lives, like a cat.

TYSEFEW
Mew! You would be taken up for that.

CRISPINELLA
Nay, good, let me still sit; we low statures love still to sit, lest when we stand we may be supposed to sit.

TYSEFEW
Dost not wear high cork shoes – chopines?

CRISPINELLA
Monstrous ones. I am, as many other are, pieced above and pieced beneath.

TYSEFEW
Still the best part in the –

CRISPINELLA
And yet all will scarce make me so high as one of the giants' stilts that stalks before my Lord Mayor's pageant.

97 *have my lip* i.e. kiss me

105 *taken up* i.e. hoisted on to another's back to be whipped (see following line: 'let me still sit'); quite what the humorous 'offence' is that would deserve punishment is unclear, perhaps that 'cat' (104) was slang for a whore.

106 *still* always

108 *chopines* A Spanish and Italian fashion, particularly associated with Venice.

109–10 *pieced ... beneath* added to above and below, with high shoes and a high headpiece

111 The word cut off here must be 'middle', referring to the part that is actually Crispinella and not addition, the compliment here probably overridden with a smile (see 'I forget my beauty' at 119–20).

113 The giants Gog and Magog usually figured in the civic pageantry of the annual procession to celebrate the election of the new Lord Mayor on 29 October, as mythical guardians of the city of London.

TYSEFEW

By the Lord, so; I thought 'twas for something Mistress Joyce jested at thy high insteps.

CRISPINELLA

She might well enough, and long enough, before I would be ashamed of my shortness. What I made or can mend myself I may blush at; but what nature put upon me, let her be ashamed for me, I ha' nothing to do with it. I forget my beauty.

TYSEFEW

Faith, Joyce is a foolish, bitter creature.

CRISPINELLA

A pretty, mildewed wench she is.

TYSEFEW

And fair –

CRISPINELLA

As myself.

TYSEFEW

O, you forget your beauty now.

CRISPINELLA

Troth, I never remember my beauty but as some men do religion – for controversy's sake.

BEATRICE

A motion, sister –

CRISPINELLA

Ninevy, *Julius Caesar*, *Jonas*, or *The Destruction of Jerusalem*?

BEATRICE

My love here –

CRISPINELLA

Prithee, call him not love: 'tis the drab's phrase; nor sweet honey, nor my cony, nor dear duckling: 'tis the citizen terms; but call me him –

BEATRICE

What?

CRISPINELLA

Anything. What's the motion?

122 *pretty, mildewed* i.e. her beauty stained by an acid disposition

126–7 *some . . . sake* A gibe at the Puritan taste for theological controversy.

128 *motion* proposal. Crispinella affects to take the word in another sense, as meaning 'puppet-show' and names some in the following line.

132 *drab* slut

133 *cony* i.e. my little rabbit

133–4 *citizen terms* i.e. low class terms, not fit for gentlefolk

136 *What's* ed. (what'st Q)

BEATRICE

You know this night our parents have intended solemnly to contract us; and my love, to grace the feast, hath promised a masque.

FREEVILL

You'll make one, Tysefew; and Caqueteur shall fill up a room.

TYSEFEW

'Fore heaven, well remembered! He borrowed a diamond of me last night to grace his finger in your visitation. The lying creature will swear some strange thing on it now.

Enter CAQUETEUR

CRISPINELLA

Peace, he's here. Stand close, lurk.

CAQUETEUR

Good morrow, most dear and worthy to be most wise. How does my mistress?

CRISPINELLA

Morrow, sweet servant; you glister. Prithee, let's see that stone.

CAQUETEUR

A toy, lady, I bought to please my finger.

CRISPINELLA

Why, I am more precious to you than your finger.

CAQUETEUR

Yes, or than all my body, I swear.

CRISPINELLA

Why, then, let it be bought to please me. Come, I am no professed beggar. [*She tries to snatch the ring*]

CAQUETEUR

Troth, mistress! Zoons! Forsooth, I protest!

CRISPINELLA

Nay, if you turn Protestant for such a toy –

140 *make one* be of the party

140–1 *fill up a room* join in too (i.e. for want of a better)

143 *to . . . visitation* See I.i.50–1.

145 *Stand . . . lurk* Stand aside, hide.

148 *glister* glitter, i.e. with the ring on his finger

153–4 *Come . . . beggar* i.e. come on, give to me, don't make me beg for it, it's not my trade. Crispinella tries to snatch the ring here which isn't really Caqueteur's to give, as in a much weightier exchange Franceschina tries at II.ii.72 to snatch one which isn't really Freevill's to give.

155 *Zoons* By God's wounds

156 *turn Protestant* i.e. *protest* that you will not part with it

CAQUETEUR
In good deed, la! Another time I'll give you a –

CRISPINELLA
Is this yours to give?

CAQUETEUR
O God! Forsooth, mine, quoth you? Nay, as for that –

CRISPINELLA
Now I remember, I ha' seen this on my servant Tysefew's finger.

CAQUETEUR
Such another.

CRISPINELLA
Nay, I am sure this is it.

CAQUETEUR
Troth, 'tis, forsooth. The poor fellow wanted money to pay for supper last night, and so pawned it to me. 'Tis a pawn, i'faith, or else you should have it.

TYSEFEW
[*Aside to Caqueteur*] Hark ye, thou base lying – How dares thy impudence hope to prosper! Weren't not for the privilege of this respected company, I would so bang thee!

CRISPINELLA
[*to Tysefew*] Come hither, servant. What's the matter betwixt you two?

CAQUETEUR
Nothing. [*Aside to Crispinella*] But, hark you, he did me some uncivil discourtesies last night, for which, because I should not call him to account, he desires to make me any satisfaction. The coward trembles at my very presence, but I ha' him on the hip; I'll take the forfeit on his ring.

TYSEFEW
What's that you whisper to her?

CAQUETEUR
Nothing, sir, but to satisfy her that the ring was not pawned, but only lent by you to grace my finger; and so told her I craved your pardon for being too familiar, or indeed, over-bold with your reputation.

CRISPINELLA
Yes, indeed, he did. He said you desired to make him any satisfaction for an uncivil discourtesy you did him last

162 *Such another* Another similar one
170 s.d. (*not in* Q)
176 *on the hip* i.e. in a (wrestling) lock
the forfeit . . . ring his ring in forfeiture

night, but said he had you o' the hip and would take the forfeit of your ring.

TYSEFEW

How now, ye base poltroon!

CAQUETEUR

Hold, hold! My mistress speaks by contraries.

TYSEFEW

Contraries?

CAQUETEUR

She jests, faith, only jests.

CRISPINELLA

Sir, I'll no more o' your service. You are a child; I'll give you to my nurse.

PUTIFER

And he come to me, I can tell you, as old as I am, what to do with him.

CAQUETEUR

I offer my service, forsooth.

TYSEFEW

Why, so; now every dog has his bone to gnaw on.

FREEVILL

The masque holds, Master Caqueteur.

CAQUETEUR

I am ready, sir. [*to Putifer*] Mistress, I'll dance with you. Ne'er fear, I'll grace you.

PUTIFER

I tell you, I can my singles and my doubles and my trick o' twenty, my carantapace, my traverse forward, and my falling back yet, i'faith.

BEATRICE

Mine, the provision for the night is ours.
Much must be our care; till night we leave you.
I am your servant; be not tyrannous.
Your virtue won me; faith, my love's not lust.
Good, wrong me not; my most fault is much trust.

186 *poltroon* spiritless coward

195 See Tilley D464, D470.

196 *holds* is to take place

199–201 The nurse names a number of dancing steps, with of course a sexual innuendo at 'falling back'.

200 *carantapace* i.e. coranto pace, the coranto a swift or 'running' dance to music in triple time

202 *Mine* My beloved (Freevill)
ours mine and my companions (referring to the Nurse and Crispinella)

FREEVILL

Until night only. My heart be with you! –
Farewell, sister.

CRISPINELLA

Adieu, brother. Come on, sister, for these sweetmeats.

FREEVILL

Let's meet and practise presently.

TYSEFEW

Content. We'll but fit our pumps. – [*to Caqueteur*] Come, ye pernicious vermin!

Exeunt [*all but* FREEVILL]

Enter MALHEUREUX

FREEVILL

My friend, wished hours! What news from Babylon?
How does the woman of sin and natural concupiscence?

MALHEUREUX

The eldest child of nature ne'er beheld
So damned a creature.

FREEVILL

What! *In nova fert animus mutatas dicere formas!* Which way bears the tide?

MALHEUREUX

Dear loved sir, I find a mind courageously vicious may put on a desperate security, but can never be blessed with a firm enjoying and self-satisfaction.

FREEVILL

What passion is this, my dear Lindabrides?

207–8 ed. (*as one line* Q)

211 *fit our pumps* try on our dancing shoes

211 s.d. (*not in* Q)

213 *wished hours* i.e. now you have had your wished hours (with Franceschina) *Babylon* The Biblical city of sin, and so metaphorical for a brothel

215 *eldest . . . nature* i.e. Adam

217 *In . . . formas* 'my spirit prompts me to tell of forms changed into new things' (first line of Ovid's *Metamorphoses*, a poem about changing shapes which provides an appropriate response to this sudden change).

219–21 *a mind . . . self-satisfaction* 'A mind courageously vicious, may happily furnish it selfe with security, but shee cannot be fraught, with this selfe-ioying delight and satisfaction' (Montaigne III.ii.24).

220 *desperate security* reckless carelessness (the sin of 'despair' ceases to hope for salvation; the sin of 'security' expects it too confidently)

222 *Lindabrides* The lady beloved of the Donzel del Febo in *The First Part of the Mirrour of Princely deedes and Knighthood*, an extravagant romance Englished from the Spanish of Diego Ortuñez de Calahorra in 1578.

MALHEUREUX

'Tis well we both may jest. I ha' been tempted to your death.

FREEVILL

What, is the rampant cockatrice grown mad for the loss of her man?

MALHEUREUX

Devilishly mad.

FREEVILL

As most assured of my second love?

MALHEUREUX

Right.

FREEVILL

She would have had this ring.

MALHEUREUX

Ay, and this heart; and in true proof you were slain, I should bring her this ring, from which she was assured you would not part until from life you parted. For which deed, and only for which deed, I should possess her sweetness.

FREEVILL

O bloody villainess! Nothing is defamed but by his proper self. Physicians abuse remedies, lawyers spoil the law, and women only shame women. You ha' vowed my death?

MALHEUREUX

My lust, not I, before my reason would. Yet I must use her. That I, a man of sense, should conceive endless pleasure in a body whose soul I know to be so hideously black!

FREEVILL

That a man at twenty-three should cry, 'O sweet pleasure!' and at forty-three should sigh, 'O sharp pox!' But consider man furnished with omnipotency, and you overthrow him. Thou must cool thy impatient appetite. 'Tis fate, 'tis fate!

226 *man* ed. (men Q)

227 *Devilishly* Diabolically

232–3 *you would . . . parted* ed. (*as one line of verse* Q)

235 *villainess* ed. (villaines Q)

238 *use* have the sexual use of

242–3 *But . . . him* Freevill comforts Malheureux with the thought that the difficulties he is in are an assurance of his human condition. 'Conceive man accompanied with omnipotency, you overwhelm him: he must in begging manner crave some empeachment and resistance of you' (Montaigne III.vii.188). Montaigne argues that great power removes a man too much from the society of his fellows, that omnipotence deprives him of humanity, which he must find again in impediments to his power.

MALHEUREUX

I do malign my creation that I am subject to passion. I must enjoy her.

FREEVILL

I have it; mark: I give a masque tonight
To my love's kindred. In that thou shalt go;
In that we two make show of falling out,
Give seeming challenge, instantly depart
With some suspicion to present fight.
We will be seen as going to our swords;
And after meeting, this ring only lent,
I'll lurk in some obscure place till rumour,
The common bawd to loose suspicions,
Have feigned me slain, which – in respect myself
Will not be found, and our late seeming quarrel –
Will quickly sound to all as earnest truth.
Then to thy wench; protest me surely dead,
Show her this ring, enjoy her, and, blood cold,
We'll laugh at folly.

MALHEUREUX O, but think of it!

FREEVILL

Think of it! Come, away! Virtue, let sleep thy passions;
What old times held as crimes are now but fashions.

Exeunt

245 *malign* slander
creation i.e. in God's image
250 *Give . . . challenge* Seem to challenge one another
251 *present* immediate
256 *in respect* as a consequence of the fact that
259 *protest* assert, proclaim
263 *'Quae fuerunt vitia, mores sunt'* (Seneca, *Epistolae*, xxxix.6, quoted by Montaigne III.ii.25).

[Act III, Scene ii]

Enter MASTER [BURNISH] *and* LIONEL; MASTER MULLIGRUB *with a standing cup in his hand, and an obligation in the other.* COCLEDEMOY *stands at the other door, disguised like a French pedlar, and overhears them*

MULLIGRUB
I am not at this time furnished, but there's my bond for your plate.

BURNISH
Your bill had been sufficient; y'are a good man. A standing cup parcel-gilt, of thirty-two ounces, eleven pound, seven shillings, the first of July. Good plate, good man, good day, good all!

MULLIGRUB
'Tis my hard fortune; I will hang the knave. No, first he shall half rot in fetters in the dungeon, his conscience made despairful. I'll hire a knave o' purpose shall assure him he is damned, and after see him with mine own eyes hanged without singing any psalm. Lord, that he has but one neck!

BURNISH
You are too tyrannous. You'll use me no further?

MULLIGRUB
No, sir; lend me your servant only, to carry the plate home. I have occasion of an hour's absence.

BURNISH
With easy consent, sir. [*to Lionel*] Haste, and be careful.
Exit

MULLIGRUB
Be very careful, I pray thee – to my wife's own hands.

LIONEL
Secure yourself, sir.

0 s.d.1 BURNISH ed. (*Garnish* Q, *but in Dramatis Personae* Burnish*; so corrected hereafter*)
0 s.d.2 *standing cup* chalice cup with a stem and base
0 s.d.3 *obligation* bond
1 *furnished* provided (with money)
3 *bill* i.e. a less elaborate acknowledgement of debt (a written order to pay a sum on a certain date)
good solvent
4 *parcel-gilt* partly gilded (on the inner surface)
11 *singing . . . psalm* any singing of a psalm
18 *Secure yourself* Be confident

MULLIGRUB

To her own hand!

LIONEL

Fear not; I have delivered greater things than this to a woman's own hand. *Exit*

COCLEDEMOY

Monsieur, please you to buy a fine delicate ball, sweet ball, a camphor ball?

MULLIGRUB

Prithee, away!

COCLEDEMOY

One-a ball to scour, a scouring ball, a ball to be shaved?

MULLIGRUB

For the love of God, talk not of shaving! I have been shaved – mischief and a thousand devils seize him! – I have been shaved. *Exit*

COCLEDEMOY

The fox grows fat when he is cursed. I'll shave ye smoother yet! Turd on a tile-stone! my lips have a kind of rheum at this bowl – I'll have't! I'll gargalize my throat with this vintner, and when I have done with him, spit him out. I'll shark! Conscience does not repine. Were I to bite an honest gentleman, a poor grogaran poet, or a penurious parson that had but ten pigs' tails in a twelvemonth, and for want of learning had but one good stool in a fortnight, I were damned beyond the works of supererogation! But to wring the withers of my gouty, barmed, spigot-frigging jumbler of elements, Mulligrub, I hold it as lawful as

20–1 *I . . . hand* With a sexual innuendo to do with erection

22 *ball* i.e. of soap (see II.iii.67–8)

25 *to be shaved* for shaving with

29 *The . . . cursed* Tilley F632

30 *my . . . rheum* my mouth waters

31 *gargalize* gargle

34 *grogaran* grogram, a coarse cheap material

34–6 *penurious . . . fortnight* an ill-educated parson and so in a parish so poor that it does not even afford him a tithing pig, but just the tails, and so starves him into constipation

37 *works . . . supererogation* In Catholic theology, good deeds done by the devout beyond what is necessary for their salvation. Cocledemoy is saying that he would be 'damned and to spare' just as they are 'saved and to spare'.

38 *withers* ridge between a horse's shoulder-blades, the part that takes the strain of the collar

barmed frothy ('barm' is the froth on fermenting liquor)

38–9 *spigot . . . elements* i.e. he fiddles with ('frigs') the tap ('spigot') of his casks while adulterating the drink with other liquid to make it go further. The sexual innuendo is also clear: 'frigging' was usual slang for masturbation.

sheep-shearing, taking eggs from hens, caudles from asses, or buttered shrimps from horses – they make no use of them, were not provided for them. And therefore, worshipful Cocledemoy, hang toasts! On, in grace and virtue to proceed! Only beware, beware degrees. There be rounds in a ladder and knots in a halter; 'ware carts. Hang toasts! the Common Council has decreed it. I must draw a lot for the great goblet. *Exit*

[Act III, Scene iii]

Enter MISTRESS MULLIGRUB *and* LIONEL *with a goblet*

[MISTRESS] MULLIGRUB

Nay, I pray you, stay and drink. And how does your mistress? I know her very well; I have been inward with her, and so has many more. She was ever a good, patient creature, i'faith. With all my heart, I'll remember your master, an honest man; he knew me before I was married. An honest man he is, and a crafty. He comes forward in the world well, I warrant him; and his wife is a proper woman, that she is. Well, she has been as proper a woman as any in Cheap; she paints now, and yet she keeps her husband's old customers to him still. In troth, a fine-faced wife in a wainscot carved seat is a worthy ornament to a tradesman's shop, and an attractive, I warrant; her husband shall

40 *caudles* warm medicinal drinks

43–4 *in ... proceed* This sounds like a verbal formula used when a student 'proceeded' to a degree; hence the following sentence.

44 *Only ... degrees* The 'degrees' Cocledemoy must beware are the steps in the ladder taking him up to the scaffold to be hanged for theft.

45 *rounds* rungs

carts criminals were taken to execution in a cart

46 *Common Council* See II.iii.79 & n. Here it is Cocledemoy's own 'common sense' which has 'decreed' his action (with a chime on 'degrees').

1 s.p. MISTRESS 1633 (*not in* Q)

2 *inward* intimate (with a following sexual innuendo)

5 *knew me* With a sexual innuendo.

5–6 *honest ... crafty* The two adjectives go strikingly together.

6 *comes forward* prospers (with sexual innuendo about erection)

7 *proper* decent; properly a woman (i.e. well capable of sex)

9 *Cheap* Cheapside (not an area known for its propriety)

paints now repairs the ravages of time by painting her face

9–10 *keeps ... him* By what means we may guess.

11–12 *tradesman's* ed. (Tradesman Q)

find it in the custom of his ware, I'll assure him. God be with you, good youth. I acknowledge the receipt.

Exit LIONEL

I acknowledge all the receipt. Sure, 'tis very well spoken! 'I acknowledge the receipt!' Thus 'tis to have good education and to be brought up in a tavern. I do keep as gallant and as good company, though I say it, as any she in London. Squires, gentlemen, and knights diet at my table, and I do lend some of them money; and full many fine men go upon my score, as simple as I stand here, and I trust them; and truly they very knightly and courtly promise fair, give me very good words, and a piece of flesh when time of year serves. Nay, though my husband be a citizen and's cap's made of wool, yet I ha' wit and can see my good as soon as another; for I have all the thanks. My silly husband, alas, he knows nothing of it; 'tis I that bear – 'tis I that must bear a brain for all.

Enter COCLEDEMOY

COCLEDEMOY

Fair hour to you, mistress!

MISTRESS MULLIGRUB

[*Aside*] 'Fair hour'! fine term; faith, I'll score it up anon. [*to Cocledemoy*] A beautiful thought to you, sir.

COCLEDEMOY

Your husband, and my master, Master Burnish, has sent you a jowl of fresh salmon; and they both will come to dinner to season your new cup with the best wine; which cup your husband entreats you to send back by me that his arms may be graved o' the side, which he forgot before it was sent.

13 *custom . . . ware* the way his wares (i.e. both his goods and his wife) attract custom

19 *diet* eat (but see I.ii.25n)

21 *score* tally of debt (and with the sense that she has 'notched them up' as sexual partners)

23–4 *a piece . . . serves* i.e. game in season, with a sexual innuendo to 'piece of flesh'

25 *cap's . . . wool* See II.ii.31n.

27 *silly* foolish, simple-minded
that bear With a sexual innuendo

30 *score it up* note it down

33 *jowl* head and shoulders

36 *arms* This is a jokey pretence at the heraldic 'arms' of a gentleman, of course, since Mulligrub is a tradesman.

[MISTRESS] MULLIGRUB

By what token? Are you sent by no token? Nay, I have wit.

COCLEDEMOY

He sent me by the same token that he was dry-shaved this morning.

MISTRESS MULLIGRUB

A sad token, but true. Here, sir. [*gives the cup*] I pray you commend me to your master, but especially to your mistress. Tell them they shall be most sincerely welcome.

Exit

COCLEDEMOY

Shall be most sincerely welcome! Worshipful Cocledemoy, lurk close. Hang toasts! Be not ashamed of thy quality! Every man's turd smells well in's own nose. Vanish, foist!

Exit

Enter MISTRESS MULLIGRUB *with Roger, Christian, other Servants and furniture for the table*

MISTRESS MULLIGRUB

Come, spread these table diaper napkins and – do you hear? – perfume! This parlour does so smell of profane tobacco. I could never endure this ungodly tobacco since one of our elders assured me, upon his knowledge, tobacco was not used in the congregation of the Family of Love. – Spread, spread handsomely! – Lord, these boys do things arsy-varsy! – You show your bringing up! I was a gentlewoman by my sister's side; I can tell ye so methodically. Methodically – I wonder where I got that word. O, Sir Aminadab Ruth bade me kiss him methodically! I had it somewhere, and I had it indeed.

38 s.p. MISTRESS 1633 (*Mr.* Q)
I have wit i.e. I'm not a fool

39 *dry-shaved* cheated, gulled, stripped clean (and by a 'barber')

46 *Every . . . nose 'Stercus cuique suum bene olet'* (Erasmus, *Adagia* II.cent iv. ad 2, quoted by Montaigne III.viii.202).
foist rogue, roguery; stench

46 s.d.2 *Roger, Christian, other* (*not in* Q)

47 *diaper* patterned linen

48–9 *profane tobacco* Satirises the well-known Puritan hatred of tobacco.

53 *arsy-varsy* topsy-turvy

54 *methodically* by an orderly proceeding. She had this new word (of the kind Marston was rather fond of) from Florio's Montaigne III.viii.200: 'to speake orderly, methodically, wisely and sufficiently, few can doe it.'

56 *Aminadab Ruth* The Biblical names (from the book of Ruth) are meant to suggest a Puritan.
had it with a sexual innuendo

Enter MASTER MULLIGRUB

MULLIGRUB

Mind, be not desperate; I'll recover all. All things with me shall seem honest that can be profitable.
He must ne'er wince, that would or thrive or save,
To be called niggard, cuckold, cut-throat, knave.

MISTRESS MULLIGRUB

Are they come, husband?

MULLIGRUB

Who? What? How now, what feast towards in my private parlour?

MISTRESS MULLIGRUB

Pray leave your foolery. What, are they come?

MULLIGRUB

Come? Who come?

MISTRESS MULLIGRUB

You need not make't so strange.

MULLIGRUB

Strange?

MISTRESS MULLIGRUB

Ay, strange. You know no man that sent me word that he and his wife would come to dinner to me, and sent this jowl of fresh salmon beforehand?

MULLIGRUB

Peace, not I! Peace! The messenger hath mistaken the house; let's eat it up quickly before it be enquired for. Sit to it! Some vinegar, quick! Some good luck yet. Faith, I never tasted salmon relished better. O, when a man feeds at other men's cost!

MISTRESS MULLIGRUB

Other men's cost? Why, did not you send this jowl of salmon?

MULLIGRUB

No.

MISTRESS MULLIGRUB

By Master Burnish' man?

MULLIGRUB

No.

58–9 ed. (Mind . . . all. / All . . . profitable, Q)

60 *wince* ed. (winch Q)

63 *towards* in preparation

75–6 *feeds . . . cost* '*Diogenes* answered according to my humor, when being demanded what kinde of Wine he liked best: *Another mans*, said he' (Montaigne III.ix.232).

MISTRESS MULLIGRUB

Sending me word that he and his wife would come to dinner to me?

MULLIGRUB

No, no.

MISTRESS MULLIGRUB

To season my new bowl?

MULLIGRUB

Bowl!

MISTRESS MULLIGRUB

And withal willed me to send the bowl back?

MULLIGRUB

Back!

MISTRESS MULLIGRUB

That you might have your arms graved on the side?

MULLIGRUB

Ha?

MISTRESS MULLIGRUB

By the same token you were dry-shaven this morning before you went forth?

MULLIGRUB

Pah! how this salmon stinks!

MISTRESS MULLIGRUB

And thereupon sent the bowl back, prepared dinner – nay, and I bear not a brain!

MULLIGRUB

Wife, do not vex me! Is the bowl gone? Is it delivered?

MISTRESS MULLIGRUB

Delivered? Yes, sure, 'tis delivered.

MULLIGRUB

I will never more say my prayers! Do not make me mad. 'Tis common! Let me not cry like a woman! Is it gone?

MISTRESS MULLIGRUB

Gone! God is my witness, I delivered it with no more intention to be cozened on't than the child new born; and yet –

MULLIGRUB

Look to my house! I am haunted with evil spirits! Hear me; do hear me! If I have not my goblet again, heaven, I'll to the devil; I'll to a conjurer! Look to my house! I'll raise all the wise men i' the street. [*Exit*]

100 *God* 1633 (Good Q)

101 *cozened on't* cheated of it

103–4 *Hear . . . hear me* ed. (here mee, doe; heare me Q)

MISTRESS MULLIGRUB

Deliver us! What words are these? I trust in God he is but drunk, sure.

Enter COCLEDEMOY

COCLEDEMOY

[*Aside*] I must have the salmon, too. Worshipful Cocledemoy, now for the masterpiece! God bless thy neck-piece, and foutra! [*to Mistress Mulligrub*] Fair mistress, my master –

MISTRESS MULLIGRUB

Have I caught you! – [*to Servant*] What, Roger!

COCLEDEMOY

Peace, good mistress. I'll tell you all. A jest, a very mere jest! Your husband only took sport to fright you. The bowl's at my master's; and there is your husband, who sent me in all haste, lest you should be over-frighted with his feigning, to come to dinner to him –

MISTRESS MULLIGRUB

Praise heaven it is no worse!

COCLEDEMOY

And desired me to desire you to send the jowl of salmon before, and yourself to come after to them; my mistress would be right glad to see you.

MISTRESS MULLIGRUB

I pray carry it. Now thank them entirely. Bless me, I was never so out of my skin in my life! Pray thank your mistress most entirely.

COCLEDEMOY

[*Aside*] So now, figo! worshipful Moll Faugh and I will munch. Cheaters and bawds go together like washing and wringing. *Exit*

MISTRESS MULLIGRUB

Beshrew his heart for his labour! How everything about me quivers! [*to Servant*] What, Christian, my hat and apron.

109–10 *too. Worshipful Cocledemoy* ed. (to, worship: *Cocledemoy* Q)
111 *neck-piece* neck (i.e. keep it from hanging)
115 *took sport* played a trick
118 *to come* to invite you to come
121 *before* on ahead
124 *out . . . skin* i.e. scared out of my wits
126 *figo* i.e. fuck you (from the gesture of putting the thumb between the first two fingers; from the Italian *fica* = fig, and thus cock)
129 *Beshrew* Curse
130 *apron* 1633 (aporne Q); decorative outer garment

Here, take my sleeves. – And how I tremble! So, I'll gossip it now for't, that's certain. Here has been revolutions and false fires indeed.

Enter MULLIGRUB

MULLIGRUB
Whither now? What's the matter with you now? Whither are you a-gadding?

MISTRESS MULLIGRUB
Come, come, play the fool no more; will you go?

MULLIGRUB
Whither, in the rank name of madness, whither?

MISTRESS MULLIGRUB
Whither? Why, to Master Burnish, to eat the jowl of salmon. Lord, how strange you make it!

MULLIGRUB
Why so? why so?

MISTRESS MULLIGRUB
Why so! Why, did not you send the selfsame fellow for the jowl of salmon that had the cup?

MULLIGRUB
'Tis well, 'tis very well.

MISTRESS MULLIGRUB
And willed me to come and eat it with you at the goldsmith's?

MULLIGRUB
O, ay, ay, ay. Art in thy right wits?

MISTRESS MULLIGRUB
Do you hear? Make a fool of somebody else! And you make an ass of me, I'll make an ox of you – do ye see?

MULLIGRUB
Nay, wife, be patient; for, look you, I may be mad, or drunk, or so; for my own part, though you can bear more than I, yet I can do well. I will not curse nor cry, but heaven knows what I think. Come, let's go hear some music; I will never more say my prayers. Let's go hear some doleful music. Nay, if heaven forget to prosper

131 *sleeves* often separate articles of dress
131–2 *gossip it* join in (at the dinner)
132 *revolutions* sudden turns
148 *make . . . you* i.e. give you horns, cuckold you
151 *cry* ed. (cary Q)

knaves, I'll go no more to the synagogue. Now I am discontented, I'll turn sectary; that is fashion.

Exeunt

Act IV, Scene i

Enter SIR HUBERT SUBBOYS, SIR LIONEL FREEVILL, CRISPINELLA, [*Ladies and Gentlemen*], *Servants with lights*

SIR HUBERT
More lights! Welcome, Sir Lionel Freevill, brother Freevill shortly. – Look to your lights!

SERVANT
The masquers are at hand.

SIR [HUBERT]
Call down our daughter. Hark, they are at hand! Rank handsomely.

Enter the Masquers, [*including among them* FREEVILL, TYSEFEW, *and* CAQUETEUR*; as*] *they dance,* [BEATRICE *enters.*

The formal dancing over, the Masquers choose partners among the guests for ordinary dancing, FREEVILL *choosing* BEATRICE.]

Enter MALHEUREUX *and takes* BEATRICE *from* FREEVILL. *They draw.*

FREEVILL
Know, sir, I have the advantage of the place;
You are not safe. I would deal even with you.

MALHEUREUX
So.

They exchange gloves as pledges

155 *synagogue* Puritan chapel (this word was used as having more Scriptural authority)

156 *sectary* i.e. become a religious extremist (the Puritan would already have been considered by most an extremist, but the humour is that every man supposes the position more extreme than his is heterodox sectarianism)

1–2 *brother . . . shortly* i.e. because of the marriage

4 s.p. HUBERT ed. (*Lyo.* Q)

4–5 *Rank handsomely* Take your places well (for the dance)

5 s.d.7 *takes* 1633 (*take* Q)

6 *I . . . place* i.e. I am among my friends and relations here

7 *even* equitably, fairly

FREEVILL
So.

BEATRICE
I do beseech you, sweet, do not for me
Provoke your fortune.

SIR LIONEL
What sudden flaw is risen?

SIR HUBERT
From whence comes this?

FREEVILL
An ulcer long time lurking now is burst.

SIR HUBERT
Good sir, the time and your designs are soft.

BEATRICE
Ay, dear sir, counsel him, advise him; 'twill relish well from your carving. – Good, my sweet, rest safe.

FREEVILL
All's well, all's well. This shall be ended straight.

SIR HUBERT
The banquet stays; there we'll discourse more large.

FREEVILL
Marriage must not make men cowards.

SIR LIONEL
Nor rage fools.

SIR HUBERT
'Tis valour not where heat, but reason rules.

Ex[eunt.] Only TYSEFEW *and* CRISPINELLA *stay*

TYSEFEW
But do you hear, lady, you proud ape, you;
What was the jest you brake of me even now?

CRISPINELLA
Nothing. I only said you were all mettle, that you had a brazen face, a leaden brain, and a copper beard.

TYSEFEW
Quicksilver! thou little more than a dwarf, and something less than a woman.

10–11 ed. (*as prose* Q)
14 *soft* i.e. gentle, peaceable
18 *stays* is waiting
20 s.d. *Exeunt* 1633 (*Exit* Q)
22 *brake of* made about
23 *mettle* spirit (with a pun on 'metal'; the metals that follow each also have a metaphorical meaning: 'brazen' = shameless, 'leaden' = dull, 'copper'= sham, pretentious; also, red. Marston himself is said to have had a red beard)
25 *Quicksilver* Tysefew in his turn uses a metal to comment on the speed of Crispinella's wit.
25–6 *something . . . woman* Perhaps a glance at the fact that a boy is playing the part.

CRISPINELLA

A wisp, a wisp, a wisp! Will you go to the banquet?

TYSEFEW

By the Lord, I think thou wilt marry shortly, too; thou growest somewhat foolish already.

CRISPINELLA

O, i'faith, 'tis a fair thing to be married, and a necessary. To hear this word *must*! If our husbands be proud, we must bear his contempt; if noisome, we must bear with the goat under his armholes; if a fool, we must bear his babble; and, which is worse, if a loose liver, we must live upon unwholesome reversions. Where, on the contrary side, our husbands – because they *may*, and we *must* – care not for us. Things hoped with fear and got with strugglings are men's high pleasures when duty pales and flats their appetite.

TYSEFEW

What a tart monkey is this! By heaven, if thou hadst not so much wit, I could find in my heart to marry thee. Faith, bear with me for all this.

CRISPINELLA

Bear with thee? I wonder how thy mother could bear thee ten months in her belly when I cannot endure thee two hours in mine eye.

TYSEFEW

Alas for you, sweet soul! By the Lord, you are grown a proud, scurvy, apish, idle, disdainful, scoffing – God's foot! because you have read *Euphues and his England*, *Palmerin de Oliva*, and the *Legend of Lies*!

27 *A wisp* i.e. a mere nothing

31 *must* Q(c) (must Q(u))

32 *noisome* smelly

33–4 *babble* foolish chatter

35 *unwholesome reversions* i.e. 'inherit' from our husband the pox he has acquired from a whore

38 *duty* i.e. the dutiful sex possible with a wife
pales . . . flats weakens and dulls

41 *to* 1633 (to my Q)

43 Crispinella allows Tysefew's phrase (= put up with me) to drift towards 'have a child by you'.

48 *Euphues* Q(c) (*Ephius* Q(u))

48–9 *you . . . Lies* i.e. you are up-to-date with the latest romantic fiction: the 1580 sequel to John Lyly's *Euphues: the Anatomy of Wit* (1578); one of the novels in the series translated by Anthony Munday from 1588 onwards under the general title *The Mirror of Knighthood*; and Tysefew's own generic title for any romantic twaddle.

CRISPINELLA

Why, i'faith, yet, servant, you of all others should bear with my known unmalicious humours. I have always in my heart given you your due respect, and, heaven may be sworn, I have privately given fair speech of you, and protested –

TYSEFEW

Nay, look you, for my own part, if I have not as religiously vowed my heart to you, been drunk to your health, swallowed flapdragons, eat glasses, drunk urine, stabbed arms, and done all the offices of protested gallantry for your sake; and yet you tell me I have a brazen face, a leaden brain, and a copper beard! Come, yet, and it please you.

CRISPINELLA

No, no, you do not love me.

TYSEFEW

By —, but I do now; and whosoever dares say that I do not love you, nay, honour you, and if you would vouchsafe to marry –

CRISPINELLA

Nay, as for that, think on't as you will, but God's my record – and my sister knows I have taken drink and slept upon't – that if ever I marry it shall be you; and I will marry, and yet I hope I do not say it shall be you neither.

TYSEFEW

By heaven, I shall be as soon weary of health as of your enjoying! Will you cast a smooth cheek upon me?

52–4 ed. (Hart ... respect: / And ... protested. Q)

56–7 *swallowed flapdragons* 'a game, probably of Dutch origin, in which raisins, or even candle-ends, were set aflame in brandy and then swallowed still burning' (Wine, and see II.ii.16). The point is, of course, that these are not the 'real' dragons of romance; nor are any of Tysefew's feats of 'protested gallantry' quite up to the standard of the *Legend of Lies*, even though lovers do at times seem to have done such things.

57 *stabbed arms* i.e. to let the blood drip into wine, which the lover then drank

62 *By*— ed. (By ( ) Q). As Davison remarks, the brackets in Q at this point can hardly indicate a censored oath, since the rest of the play is so full of them. His suggestion that some stage business is indicated is interesting; but it may equally be that at this point Tysefew finds oaths and wit fail him and allow instead the simple protestation of love.

66 *taken drink* pledged in wine

66–7 *taken ... upon't* i.e. decided calmly, not in the heat of the moment

70 *cast ... cheek* look favourably

CRISPINELLA

I cannot tell. I have no crumped shoulders, my back needs no mantle; and yet marriage is honourable. Do you think ye shall prove a cuckold?

TYSEFEW

No, by the Lord, not I!

CRISPINELLA

Why, I thank you, i'faith. Heigh-ho! I slept on my back this morning and dreamt the strangest dreams. Good Lord, how things will come to pass! Will you go to the banquet?

TYSEFEW

If you will be mine, you shall be your own. My purse, my body, my heart is yours; only be silent in my house, modest at my table, and wanton in my bed, and the Empress of Europe cannot content, and shall not be contented, better.

CRISPINELLA

Can any kind heart speak more discreetly affectionately! My father's consent, and as for mine –

TYSEFEW

Then thus, and thus, so Hymen should begin;
[*He kisses her*]
Sometimes a falling out proves falling in.

Ex[*eunt*]

71–2 *needs no mantle* i.e. to cover the 'crumped shoulders' of a hunchback

72 *and ... honourable* i.e. and not only a refuge for a woman when she is past her best, no longer able to play the game of love; as Crispinella's next question makes plain, she is not past her best. She does have a minor obsession, however, about crooked shoulders (see III.i.94), perhaps because they were often thought to go with very short, 'dwarfish' stature like hers.

75–6 *I slept ... dreams* Both these words and the cuckold reference in Crispinella's last speech make it seem she has in mind part of the song Cocledemoy sings later (see IV.v.64–69).

75–8 ed. (Why ... yfaith: / Heigho ... morning / And ... dreames: / Good ... passe? / Will ... banquet? Q)

84 *discreetly* judiciously

86 *Hymen* marriage (from Hymen, the Greek god of marriage)

87 s.d. 1633 (*Exit.* Q)

[Act IV, Scene ii]

Enter FREEVILL, *speaking to some within;* MALHEUREUX *at the other door*

FREEVILL
As you respect my virtue, give me leave
To satisfy my reason, though not blood. –
So, all runs right; our feigned rage hath ta'en
To fullest life; they are much possessed
Of force most, most all quarrel. Now, my right friend,
Resolve me with open breast, free and true heart,
Cannot thy virtue, having space to think
And fortify her weakened powers with reason,
Discourses, meditations, discipline,
Divine ejaculatories, and all those aids against devils –
Cannot all these curb thy low appetite
And sensual fury?

MALHEUREUX
There is no God in blood, no reason in desire.
Shall I but live? Shall I not be forced to act
Some deed whose very name is hideous?

FREEVILL
No.

MALHEUREUX Then I must enjoy Franceschina.

FREEVILL You shall:
I'll lend this ring; show it to that fair devil.
It will resolve me dead;
Which rumour, with my artificial absence,
Will make most firm. Enjoy her suddenly!

2 *though not blood* even if not my passion

3–4 *hath ... life* has been entirely accepted as genuine

4–5 *they ... quarrel* The best that can be done with the sense of these lines is an awkward paraphrase: 'those who are most possessed of force (i.e. energy, spirit) mostly all quarrel'; but in reality it seems possible that a whole line has dropped out after 'possessed' – e.g. 'That in a private strife of such a kind', so that the sense becomes: 'those I have just spoken to are convinced ('possessed') that in a private quarrel like this most men must of course fight a duel'.

10 *Divine ejaculatories* Short, fervent prayers (the sexual sense of 'ejaculation' is intended to lurk here, of course, fended off by the rare use of the adjective as a quasi-noun, which cannot strictly carry the sexual sense)

14 *Shall ... live?* i.e. if I can't have her, shall I be content simply to live (rather than commit the 'hideous deed' of suicide)

16–17 *You ... devil.* (*as one line* Q)

18–20 ed. (It ... artificiall / absence ... sodainlie. Q)

19 *artificial* contrived

MALHEUREUX
But if report go strong that you are slain,
And that by me, whereon I may be seized,
Where shall I find your being?
FREEVILL
At Master Shatewe's the jeweller's, to whose breast
I'll trust our secret purpose.
MALHEUREUX Ay, rest yourself;
Each man hath follies.
FREEVILL But those worst of all,
Who with a willing eye do, seeing, fall.
MALHEUREUX
'Tis true, but truth seems folly in madness' spectacles.
I am not now myself – no man. Farewell.
FREEVILL Farewell.
MALHEUREUX
When woman's in the heart, in the soul hell. *Exit*
FREEVILL
Now repentance, the fool's whip, seize thee!
Nay, if there be no means, I'll be thy friend,
But not thy vice's; and with greatest sense
I'll force thee feel thy errors to the worst.
The vilest of dangers thou shalt sink into.
No jeweller shall see me; I will lurk
Where none shall know or think; close I'll withdraw
And leave thee with two friends – a whore and knave.
But is this virtue in me? No, not pure;
Nothing extremely best with us endures.
No use in simple purities; the elements
Are mixed for use. Silver without alloy
Is all too eager to be wrought for use:

25–6 *Ay . . . follies.* ed. (*as one line* Q)

27 See II.ii.225.

32 *no means* i.e. no other possible course of action for me

33 *with . . . sense* i.e. in the most feeling way possible

35 *vilest* (vildest Q)

37 *close* i.e. into a secret place

38 *knave* i.e. Freevill in disguise as Don Dubon and a pander (see IV.iv.33 and V.i.84). It is tempting to follow Jackson and Neill in reversing the last two nouns of this line for the rhyme.

39–45 'The weaknes of our condition, causeth, that things in their naturall simplicitie and puritie cannot fall into our use . . . Metals likewise, yea golde must be empaired with some other stuffe to make it fit for our service. Nor vertue so simple . . . hath beene able to doe no good without composition' (Montaigne II.xx.498).

43 *eager* brittle

Nor precise virtues, ever purely good,
Holds useful size with temper of weak blood.
Then let my course be borne, though with side wind,
The end being good, the means are well assigned. *Exit*

[Act IV, Scene iii]

Enter FRANCESCHINA *melancholy,* COCLEDEMOY *leading her*

COCLEDEMOY

Come, cacafuego, Frank o' Frank Hall! Who, who, ho! Excellent! Ha, here's a plump-rumped wench, with a breast softer than a courtier's tongue, an old lady's gums, or an old man's *mentula.* My fine rogue –

FRANCESCHINA

Pah, you poltroon!

COCLEDEMOY

Goody fist, flumpum pumpum! Ah, my fine wagtail, thou art as false, as prostituted, and adulterate, as some translated manuscript. Buss, fair whore, buss!

FRANCESCHINA

God's sacrament, pox!

COCLEDEMOY

Hadamoy key, dost thou frown, *medianthon teukey*? Nay, look here. *Numeron key,* silver *blithefor cany, os cany* goblet: *us key ne moy blegefoy oteeston* pox on you, gosling!

44 *precise* rigorous, over-nice (a Puritan was sometimes called a 'precisian')
ever always

45 i.e. are usefully proportioned to a temperament weakened by passion

46 *borne* held to (the sailing metaphor is of sailing ahead using a wind on the beam)

1–12 1633 (*as irregular verse* Q)

1 *cacafuego* spitfire (Lat. *cacare* = to shit; Sp. *fuego* = fire)
Frank o' Frank Hall See II.i.155n.

4 *mentula* Rather literary Latin slang for 'cock'

6 *wagtail* The bird-image is used to mean a whore (see OED Tail = buttocks sb[1] 5; also 'gosling' at 12 and 'up-tail' at 16). See also V.iii.3–4.

7 *adulterate* 1633 (adulcerate Q). The spelling of Q here preserves a no doubt intended chime with 'ulcerate'.

7–8 *translated manuscript* A scholar's sort of image from Cocledemoy (part of his usual style, see II.i.163n), which leads into his gabble of nonsense Greek in the next lines, as with the Greek and the stolen goblet and the general energy of his speech he tries to get Franceschina into bed.

FRANCESCHINA

By me fait, dis bin very fine langage. Ick sall bush ye now! Ha, be garzon, vare had you dat plate?

COCLEDEMOY

Hedemoy key, get you gone, punk rampant, *key*, common up-tail!

Enter MARY FAUGH *in haste*

MARY FAUGH

O, daughter, cousin, niece, servant, mistress!

COCLEDEMOY

Humpum plumpum squat, I am gone. *Exit*

MARY FAUGH

There is one Master Malheureux at the door desires to see you. He says he must not be denied, for he hath sent you this ring, and withal says 'tis done.

FRANCESCHINA

Vat sall me do now, God's sacrament! Tell him two hours hence he sall be most affectionately velcome. Tell him (vat sall me do?) – tell him ick am bin in my bate, and ick sall perfume my seets, mak-a mine body so delicate for his arm, two hours hence.

MARY FAUGH

I shall satisfy him; two hours hence, well. *Exit*

FRANCESCHINA

Now ick sall revange! Hay, begar! me sall tartar de whole generation! Mine brain vork it. Freevill is dead; Malheureux sall hang; and mine rival, Beatrice, ick sall make run mad.

Enter MARY FAUGH

13 *bush* kiss (she has just seen the goblet)
14 *be garzon* by God's wounds
15 *punk rampant* As at II.ii.84.
21 *withal* besides
24 *bate* bath
25 *seets* sheets
delicate delicious. See II.i.167n.
28 *tartar* torture
29–31 *Freevill* . . . *mad.* 1633 (*Frevile* . . . hang, / *A*nd . . . madde. Q)

MARY FAUGH

He's gone, forsooth, to eat a caudle of cock-stones, and will return within this two hours.

FRANCESCHINA

Very vell. Give monies to some fellow to squire me; ick sall go abroad.

MARY FAUGH

There's a lusty bravo beneath, a stranger, but a good stale rascal. He swears valiantly, kicks a bawd right virtuously, and protests with an empty pocket right desperately. He'll squire you.

FRANCESCHINA

Very velcome. Mine fan! Ick sall retorn presantly.

[*Exit* MARY FAUGH]

Now sall me be revange. Ten tousant devla! Dere sall be no Got in me but passion, no tought but rage, no mercy but blood, no spirit but divla in me. Dere sall noting tought good for me, but dat is mischievous for others.

Exit

[Act IV, Scene iv]

Enter SIR HUBERT, SIR LIONEL, BEATRICE, CRISPINELLA, *and* NURSE [PUTIFER], TYSEFEW *following*

SIR LIONEL

Did no one see him since? Pray God – nay, all is well. A little heat, what? He is but withdrawn. And yet I would to God – but fear you nothing.

BEATRICE

Pray God that all be well, or would I were not!

TYSEFEW

He's not to be found, sir, anywhere.

SIR LIONEL

You must not make a heavy face presage an ill event. I like

32 *caudle of cock-stones* i.e. a hot soup made of cock's testicles, as an aphrodisiac

36 *lusty bravo* fine daring villain

stranger foreigner

stale old and strong, well brewed (of liquor; OED a[1] 1, here used figuratively)

43–4 *Dere . . . others.* 1633 (Dere . . . me, / But . . . others. Q)

0 s.d.2 NURSE PUTIFER (*Nurse* Q)

1–3 1633 (Did . . . well, / A . . . God, / But . . . nothing. Q)

2 *heat* bout of bad temper

4 *were not* were dead

your sister well; she's quick and lively. Would she would marry, faith!

CRISPINELLA

Marry? nay, and I would marry, methinks an old man's a quiet thing.

SIR LIONEL

Ha, mass! and so he is.

CRISPINELLA

You are a widower?

SIR LIONEL

That I am, i'faith, fair Crispinella; and I can tell you, would you affect me, I have it in me yet, i'faith.

CRISPINELLA

Troth, I am in love. Let me see your hand. Would you cast yourself away upon me willingly?

SIR LIONEL

Will I? Ay, by the –

CRISPINELLA

Would you be a cuckold willingly? By my troth, 'tis a comely, fine, and handsome sight for one of my years to marry an old man; truth, 'tis restorative. What a comfortable thing it is to think of her husband, to hear his venerable cough o' the everlastings, to feel his rough skin, his summer hands and winter legs, his almost no eyes, and assuredly no teeth! And then to think what she must dream of when she considers others' happiness and her own want – 'tis a worthy and notorious comfortable match!

SIR LIONEL

Pish, pish! will you have me?

CRISPINELLA

Will you assure me –

SIR LIONEL

Five hundred pound jointure?

CRISPINELLA

That you will die within this fortnight?

SIR LIONEL

No, by my faith, Crispinella.

14 *I . . . yet* i.e. to satisfy you sexually

15 *Let . . . hand* A dry hand indicated age and sexual deficiency.

22 *cough . . . everlastings* everlasting cough; cough that will see him into eternity

23 *summer . . . winter* i.e. hot . . . cold

CRISPINELLA
Then Crispinella, by her faith, assures you she'll have none of you.

Enter FREEVILL, *disguised like a pander, and* FRANCESCHINA

FREEVILL
By'r leave, gentles and men of nightcaps, I would speak, but that here stands one is able to express her own tale best.

FRANCESCHINA
Sir, mine speech is to you. You had a son, Matre Freevill?

SIR LIONEL
Had, ha, and have!

FRANCESCHINA
No point; me am come to assure you dat one Mestre Malheureux hath killed him.

BEATRICE
O me! wretched, wretched!

SIR HUBERT
Look to our daughter.

SIR LIONEL
How art thou informed?

FRANCESCHINA
If dat it please you to go vid me, ick sall bring you where you sall hear Malheureux vid his own lips confess it; and dere ye may apprehend him, and revenge your and mine love's blood.

SIR HUBERT
Your love's blood, mistress? Was he your love?

FRANCESCHINA
He was so, sir; let your daughter hear it. – Do not veep, lady. De yong man dat be slain did not love you, for he still lovit me ten tousant tousant times more dearly.

BEATRICE
O my heart! I will love you the better; I cannot hate what

33 s.d. *disguised . . . pander* The 'lusty bravo' of IV.iii.36 has taken on a second layer of disguise to accompany Franceschina.

34 *gentles* gentlefolk
men of nightcaps i.e. elderly men

34–6 1633 (Beere . . . speak, / But . . . best. Q)

37 *Matre* Master

39 *No point* i.e. no you have not (Fr. *point du tout* = not at all)

52–3 *I will . . . affected* Is Beatrice speaking to Franceschina or to her own heart?

he affected. O passion! O my grief! which way wilt break, think, and consume?

CRISPINELLA
Peace!

BEATRICE
Dear woes cannot speak.

FRANCESCHINA
For look you, lady, dis your ring he gave me, vid most bitter jests at your scorned kindness.

BEATRICE
He did not ill not to love me, but sure he did not well to mock me; gentle minds will pity though they cannot love. Yet peace and my love sleep with him! – Unlace, good nurse. – Alas, I was not so ambitious of so supreme an happiness that he should only love me; 'twas joy enough for me, poor soul, that I only might only love him.

FRANCESCHINA
O, but to be abused, scorned, scoffed at! O, ten tousant divla, by such a one, and unto such a one!

BEATRICE
I think you say not true. – Sister, shall we know one another in the other world?

CRISPINELLA
What means my sister?

BEATRICE
I would fain see him again. O my tortured mind!
Freevill is more than dead; he is unkind.

Ex[eunt] BEATRICE *and* CRISPINELLA *and* NURSE [PUTIFER]

SIR HUBERT
Convey her in, and so, sir, as you said,
Set a strong watch.

SIR LIONEL Ay, sir, and so pass along
With this same common woman.
[*to Franceschina*] You must make it good.

53 *wilt* 1633 (will Q)

54 *think* Beatrice's woes will be private, breaking her life in their inner consuming thought. See 56n.

56 Cf. the usual tag from Seneca, *Hippolytus*, 607: *Curae leves loquuntur, ingentes stupent* = light cares speak, great ones strike dumb.

61 *Unlace* i.e. untie the laces of my stays (to relieve the pressure of emotion). Beatrice is not, of course, asking that this shall be done on stage, but shortly retires with her sister and the nurse.

71 s.d. *Exeunt* 1633 (*Exit* Q)

73–4 ed. (*as prose* Q)

FRANCESCHINA
Ick sall, or let me pay for his, mine blood.
SIR HUBERT
Come, then, along all, with quiet speed.
SIR LIONEL
O fate!
TYSEFEW
O, sir, be wisely sorry, but not passionate.

Ex[*eunt*]; *all but* FREEVILL

FREEVILL
I will go and reveal myself. Stay! No, no!
Grief endears love. Heaven! to have such a wife
Is happiness to breed pale envy in the saints.
Thou worthy, dove-like virgin without gall,
Cannot that woman's evil, jealousy,
Despite disgrace, nay, which is worst, contempt,
Once stir thy faith? O truth, how few sisters hast thou!
Dear memory!
With what a suffering sweetness, quiet modesty,
Yet deep affection, she received my death!
And then with what a patient, yet oppressed kindness
She took my lewdly intimated wrongs!
O, the dearest of heaven!
Were there but three such women in the world,
Two might be saved. Well, I am great
With expectation to what devilish end
This woman of foul soul will drive her plots:
But providence all wicked art o'ertops,
And impudence must know, though stiff as ice,
That fortune doth not alway dote on vice. *Exit*

77 s.d. *Exeunt* ed. (*Exit* Q); *all but* (*Manet* Q)

81 *dove-like ... gall* The gentle dove or pigeon was supposed to have no gall bladder and no secretion of gall from the liver to store there, since gall was the source of bitterness and rancour.

84 *stir* shake

85–6 ed. (*as one line* Q)

89 *wrongs* i.e. wrongdoing

89–93 ed. (She ... heauen? / Were ... two / Might ... saued. / Well ... end Q)

92 *Two ... saved* i.e. because the third would quite certainly be saved, that is Beatrice; even among paragons of virtue like her, she would still stand out

96 *impudence* shamelessness
stiff unyielding, obstinate

[Act IV, Scene v]

Enter SIR HUBERT, SIR LIONEL, TYSEFEW, FRANCESCHINA, *and three* [*Constables*] *with halberds*

SIR HUBERT
Plant a watch there. Be very careful, sirs.
The rest with us.

TYSEFEW
The heavy night grows to her depth of quiet;
'Tis about mid-darkness.

FRANCESCHINA
Mine shambre is hard by; ick sall bring you to it presantment.

SIR LIONEL
Deep silence! On!

Exeunt. [*Constables remain*]

COCLEDEMOY
(*Within*) Wa, ha, ho!

Enter MULLIGRUB

MULLIGRUB
It was his voice; 'tis he! He sups with his cupping-glasses. 'Tis late; he must pass this way. I'll ha' him; I'll ha' my fine boy, my worshipful Cocledemoy. I'll moy him! He shall be hanged in lousy linen; I'll hire some sectary to make him an heretic before he die; and when he is dead, I'll piss on his grave.

Enter COCLEDEMOY

COCLEDEMOY
Ay, my fine punks, good night, Frank Frailty, Frail o' Frail Hall! *Bonus noches*, my *ubiquitari*!

5 *hard by* near by 5–6 *presantment* at once

7 s.d. ed. (*after 8* Q)

9 *He . . . cupping-glasses* i.e. he drinks with his fellow 'drawers of blood' or 'leeches' (suckers in of other men's goods); a cupping-glass was used to draw blood medicinally, like leeches, and is the preferred term here because it goes with the cups Cocledemoy and his companions are drinking from.

11 *moy* A threatening nonsense verb formed from the last syllable of Cocledemoy's name.

13 *heretic . . . die* So that he will be not only dead but damned. See II.iii.8–9n and III.iii.156n.

16 *Bonus noches* Partially latinised form of Sp. *buenos noches* = good night; 'another piece of characteristic polyglot swagger' (Jackson and Neill); *ubiquitari* i.e. the kind of people who are found everywhere (from Lat. *ubique* = everywhere)

MULLIGRUB
'Ware polling and shaving, sir!

COCLEDEMOY
A wolf, a wolf, a wolf!

Exit COCLEDEMOY, *leaving his cloak behind him*

MULLIGRUB
Here's something yet! A cloak, a cloak! Yet I'll after; he cannot 'scape the watch. I'll hang him if I have any mercy! I'll slice him! *Exit*

Enter COCLEDEMOY. [*The Constables step forward*]

[1] CONSTABLE
Who goes there? Come before the constable.

COCLEDEMOY
Bread o' God, constable, you are a watch for the devil! Honest men are robbed under your nose. There's a false knave in the habit of a vintner set upon me. He would have had my purse, but I took me to my heels. Yet he got my cloak: a plain stuff cloak, poor, yet 'twill serve to hang him! 'Tis my loss, poor man that I am! [*Exit*]

2 CONSTABLE
Masters, we must watch better. Is't not strange that knaves, drunkards, and thieves should be abroad, and yet we of the watch, scriveners, smiths, and tailors, never stir?

Enter MULLIGRUB *running with* COCLEDEMOY*'s cloak*

[1] CONSTABLE
Hark! who goes there?

MULLIGRUB
An honest man and a citizen.

2 CONSTABLE
Appear, appear! What are you?

MULLIGRUB
A simple vintner.

20 *if . . . mercy* i.e. if God in his mercy grants me this (chiming deliberately against Mulligrub's own mercilessness)

22 s.p. ed. (*Const.* Q)

23 *for the devil* i.e. on the devil's side

27 *stuff* woollen fabric

31 *scriveners . . . tailors* i.e. followers of respectable trades

31 s.d. ed. (*after 28* Q)

32 s.p. 1633 (2. Q)

1 CONSTABLE

A vintner, ha? and simple? Draw nearer, nearer. Here's the cloak!

2 CONSTABLE

Ay, Master Vintner, we know you. A plain stuff cloak: 'tis it.

1 CONSTABLE

Right, come! O, thou varlet, dost not thou know that the wicked cannot 'scape the eyes of the constable?

MULLIGRUB

What means this violence? As I am an honest man, I took the cloak –

2 CONSTABLE

As you are a knave, you took the cloak; we are your witnesses for that.

MULLIGRUB

But hear me, hear me! I'll tell you what I am.

2 CONSTABLE

A thief you are.

MULLIGRUB

I tell you my name is Mulligrub.

1 CONSTABLE

I will grub you! In with him to the stocks! There let him sit till tomorrow morning, that Justice Quodlibet may examine him.

MULLIGRUB

Why, but I tell thee –

2 CONSTABLE

Why, but I tell thee! We'll tell thee now.

[*Constables put* MULLIGRUB *in the stocks*]

MULLIGRUB

Am I not mad? Am I not an ass? Why, scabs – God's foot, let me out!

2 CONSTABLE

Ay, ay, let him prate; he shall find matter in us scabs, I warrant. God's-so, what good members of the commonwealth do we prove!

49 *grub* i.e. root you out, the verb suggested by the last syllable of Mulligrub's name
50 *Quodlibet* Whatever you please. See II.iii.17.
56 *matter . . . scabs* matter of consequence in us scoundrels (with an unconscious glance at the idea of pus in a sore)

1 CONSTABLE

Prithee, peace! Let's remember our duties, and let's go sleep in the fear of God.

Exeunt, having left MULLIGRUB *in the stocks*

MULLIGRUB

Who goes there? Illo, ho, ho! Zounds, shall I run mad, lose my wits? Shall I be hanged? – Hark, who goes there? Do not fear to be poor, Mulligrub; thou hast a sure stock now.

Enter COCLEDEMOY *like a bellman*

COCLEDEMOY

The night grows old,
And many a cuckold
Is now – Wa, ha, ha, ho!
Maids on their backs
Dream of sweet smacks
And warm – Wo, ho, ho, ho!

[*Aside*] I must go comfort my venerable Mulligrub; I must fiddle him till he fist. Fough! –

Maids in your night-rails,
Look well to your light —
Keep close your locks,
And down your smocks;
Keep a broad eye,
And a close thigh –

Excellent, excellent! – Who's there? Now, Lord, Lord – Master Mulligrub! – Deliver us! What does your worship in the stocks? I pray come out, sir.

59 *Let's* 1633 (let Q)
61 *Illo, ho, ho* cry of the falconer to lure the falcon. See I.ii.40n.
63 *stock* i.e. what he is sitting in, punning on a tradesman's stock
63 s.d. *bellman* town crier or night watchman
65–6 ed. (*as one line* Q)
68 *smacks* kisses
68–9 ed. (*as one line* Q)
70 s.d. (*not in* Q)
70–1 ed. (I must go ... must / Fiddle ... fough: Q)
70 *comfort* One of the duties of the bellman was to visit condemned criminals in prison before execution.
71 *fiddle ... fist* cheat him till he farts
72 *night-rails* night-dresses
73 *light—* ed. (light (–) Q). The rhyme word is probably 'tails', the word left blank perhaps because the audience knew the song and could supply it by joining in. See IV.iii.6n.
77–8 *And ... there?* ed. (*as one line* Q)

MULLIGRUB

Zounds, man, I tell thee I am locked!

COCLEDEMOY

Locked! O world, O men, O time, O night! that canst not discern virtue and wisdom and one of the Common Council! What is your worship in for?

MULLIGRUB

For (a plague on't!) suspicion of felony.

COCLEDEMOY

Nay, and it be but such a trifle. Lord, I could weep to see your good worship in this taking. Your worship has been a good friend to me; and, though you have forgot me, yet I knew your wife before she was married; and, since, I have found your worship's door open, and I have knocked, and God knows what I have saved. And do I live to see your worship stocked!

MULLIGRUB

Honest bellman, I perceive thou knowest me;
I prithee call the watch.
Inform the constable of my reputation,
That I may no longer abide in this shameful habitation;
And hold thee all I have about me. (*gives him his purse*)

COCLEDEMOY

'Tis more than I deserve, sir. Let me alone for your delivery.

MULLIGRUB

Do, and then let me alone with Cocledemoy. I'll moy him!

COCLEDEMOY

Maids in your –

[*Enter the Constables*]

Master Constable, who's that i'th' stocks?

1 CONSTABLE

One for a robbery, one Mulligrub he calls himself.

83–4 *one . . . Council* See II.iii.79 & n.

87 *taking* state of arrest; plight; state of alarm

89 *knew* See III.iii.5n. The open door and the knocking that follow have sexual connotations, of course, and 'saved' at 91 allows the innuendo of theft to surface as well. The literal meaning is of the bellman, in the course of his duties, finding a door open and alerting the householder by knocking, so as to safeguard his goods.

93–5 ed. (*as prose* Q)

98 *Let me alone* Trust me, have confidence in me

[COCLEDEMOY]
Mulligrub?

[1 CONSTABLE]
Bellman, knowest thou him?

COCLEDEMOY
Know him? O, Master Constable, what good service have you done! Know him! He's a strong thief; his house has been suspected for a bawdy tavern a great while, and a receipt for cutpurses, 'tis most certain. He has been long in the black book, and is he ta'en now?

2 CONSTABLE
By'r Lady, my masters, we'll not trust the stocks with him; we'll have him to the justice's, get a *mittimus* to Newgate presently. – Come, sir, come on, sir!

MULLIGRUB
Ha! does your rascalship yet know my worship in the end?

1 CONSTABLE
Ay, the end of your worship we know.

MULLIGRUB
Ha, goodman constable, here's an honest fellow can tell you what I am.

2 CONSTABLE
'Tis true, sir; y'are a strong thief, he says, on his own knowledge. Bind fast, bind fast! We know you: we'll trust no stocks with you. Away with him to the jail instantly!

MULLIGRUB
Why, but dost hear – Bellman! Rogue! Rascal! God's – why, but –

The Constable[*s drag*] *away* MULLIGRUB

104 s.p. ed. (*not in* Q, *where this response is part of the Constable's speech*)
105 s.p. ed. (*not in* Q)
107 *strong* flagrant, outrageous
108–9 *receipt for cutpurses* i.e. a place where pickpockets could exchange their stolen goods for cash
110 *black book* i.e. on the list of those who should be punished
112 *mittimus* warrant for imprisonment (from its first word in Latin: 'we send') *Newgate* A London prison
113 *presently* immediately
114 *in the end* at long last
115 *end . . . worship* i.e. the end 'your worship' is coming to, perhaps also, the end of your honourable status
116 *goodman constable* This is like trying to fend off his modern equivalent by calling him 'officer' with ingratiating condescension; 'goodman' was a form of address used to those just below the rank of gentleman, 'your worship' a peg above this.
122 s.d. *Constables drag* (*constable drags* Q)

COCLEDEMOY

Why, but! Wa, ha, ha! Excellent, excellent! Ha, my fine Cocledemoy, my vintner fists! I'll make him fart crackers before I ha' done with him. Tomorrow is the day of judgement. Afore the Lord God, my knavery grows unparegal! 'Tis time to take a nap, until half an hour hence. God give your worship music, content, and rest! *Ex*[*it*]

Act V, Scene i

Enter FRANCESCHINA, SIR LIONEL, TYSEFEW, [FREEVILL *disguised as before*], *with Officers*

FRANCESCHINA

You bin very velcome to mine shambra.

SIR LIONEL

But how know ye, how are ye assured,
Both of the deed and of his sure return?

FRANCESCHINA

O, mynheer, ick sall tell you. Mettre Malheureux came all breatless running a my shambra, his sword all bloody: he tell-a me he had kill Freevill, and prayed-a me to conceal him. Ick flatter him, bid bring monies, he should live and lie vid me. He went, whilst ick (me hope vidout sins) out of mine mush love to Freevill betray him.

SIR LIONEL

Fear not, 'tis well: good works get grace for sin.

She conceals them behind the curtain

FRANCESCHINA

Dere, peace, rest dere; so, softly, all go in.
[*Aside*] De net is lay; now sall ick be revenge.
If dat me knew a dog dat Freevill love,
Me would puisson him; for know de deepest hell
As a revenging woman's naught so fell.

124 *crackers* firecrackers
126 *unparegal* unequalled
126–8 *Afore . . . rest* 1633 (*A*fore . . . vnperegall, / Tis . . . hence: / God . . . rest Q)
128 *your worship* Cocledemoy refers to himself.
128 s.d. (*Exeunt.* Q)

4 *mynheer* Dutch equivalent of 'Sir' or 'Master'
4–9 ed. (*as irregular verse* Q)
10 *good . . . sin* A Catholic rather than Protestant view
14 *puisson* poison
15 *fell* terrible

Enter MARY FAUGH

MARY FAUGH
Ho, Cousin Frank, the party you wot of,
Master Malheureux.

FRANCESCHINA Bid him come up, I pridee.

[*Exit* MARY FAUGH]

She sings and dances to the cittern

Enter MALHEUREUX

FRANCESCHINA
O mynheer man, aderliver love,
Mine ten tousant times velcome love!
Ha, by mine trat, you bin de just – vat sall me say?
Vat seet honey name sall I call you?

MALHEUREUX Any from you
Is pleasure. Come, my loving prettiness,
Where's thy chamber? I long to touch your sheets.

FRANCESCHINA
No, no, not yet, mine seetest, soft-lipped love:
You sall not gulp down all delights at once.
Be min trat, dis all-fles-lovers, dis ravenous wenches
Dat sallow all down whole, vill have all at one bit!
Fie, fie, fie!
Be min fait, dey do eat comfits vid spoons.
No, no, I'll make you chew your pleasure vit love:
De more degrees and steps, de more delight,
De more endeared is de pleasure height.

16–17 *Ho ... Malheureux.* ed. (*as one line* Q)

17 s.d.1 (*not in* Q)

17 s.d.2 (*Cantat saltatque cum cithera.* Q); *cittern* a lute-like instrument

18 *aderliver* ed. (a dere liuer Q). Perhaps the line should be emended further to read 'O mynheer, min aderliver love'.

20 *trat* troth

21–3 ed. (Vat ... you? / *A*nie ... louing / Prettinesse ... Chamber? / I ... sheetes. Q)

26 *all-fles-lovers* i.e. who swallow all the flesh, all the meat, at once
wenches This is 'wenchers' (= one who associates with common women) in Franceschina's accented speech.

27 *sallow* swallow
bit bite

28–9 ed. (Fie ... eate / Comfets ... spoones. Q)

29 *comfits* sweets, preserved fruits
vid spoons i.e. instead of delicately, one at a time

31–2 *'The more steps and degrees there are: the more delight and honour is there on the top'* (Montaigne III.v.131).

MALHEUREUX
What, you're a learned wanton, and proceed by art!

FRANCESCHINA
Go, little vag! Pleasure should have a crane's long neck, to relish de ambrosia of delight! And ick pridee tell me, for me loves to hear of manhood very mush, i'fait. Ick pridee – vat vas me a-saying? – O, ick pridee tell-a me, how did you kill-a Mettre Freevill?

MALHEUREUX
Why, quarrelled o' set purpose, drew him out,
Singled him, and having th' advantage
Of my sword and might, ran him through and through.

FRANCESCHINA
Vat did you vid him van he was sticken?

MALHEUREUX
I dragged him by the heels to the next wharf
And spurned him in the river.

Those in ambush rusheth forth and takes him

SIR LIONEL
Seize, seize him! O monstrous! O ruthless villain!

MALHEUREUX
What mean you, gentlemen! By heaven –

TYSEFEW
Speak not of anything that's good.

MALHEUREUX
Your errors gives you passion; Freevill lives.

SIR LIONEL
Thy own lips say thou liest.

MALHEUREUX
Let me die
If at Shatewe's the jeweller he lives not safe untouched.

TYSEFEW
Meantime to strictest guard, to sharpest prison.

MALHEUREUX
No rudeness, gentlemen: I'll go undragged.

34–8 ed. (*as irregular verse* Q)

34–5 *Pleasure . . . delight* 'I wot not who in ancient time wished his throat were as long as a Cranes neck, that so hee might the longer and more leasurely taste what he swallowed' (Montaigne III.v.130).

40–1 ed. (Singled . . . sword / and might . . . through. Q)

40 *Singled* Separated him from the others (hunting term)

44 *spurned him* thrust him with my foot

48 *Your . . . passion* It is your mistake (in thinking Freevill murdered) that causes your anger.

49–50 *Let . . . untouched* ed. (*as one line* Q)

O wicked, wicked devil!

Exit [*with Officers*]

SIR LIONEL Sir, the day
Of trial is this morn. Let's prosecute
The sharpest rigour and severest end:
Good men are cruel when they're vice's friend.

SIR HUBERT
Woman, we thank thee with no empty hand; [*gives money*]
farewell.
Strumpets are fit, fit for something!

All save FREEVILL *departs*

FREEVILL
Ay, for hell!
O thou unreprievable, beyond all
Measure of grace damned immediately!
That things of beauty created for sweet use,
Soft comfort, and as the very music of life,
Custom should make so unutterably hellish!
O heaven,
What difference is in women and their life!
What man, but worthy name of man, would leave
The modest pleasures of a lawful bed,
The holy union of two equal hearts,
Mutually holding either dear as health,
The undoubted issues, joys of chaste sheets,
The unfeigned embrace of sober ignorance,
To twine the unhealthful loins of common loves,
The prostituted impudence of things
Senseless like those by cataracts of Nile,
Their use so vile takes away sense! How vile
To love a creature made of blood and hell,

53–5 *Sir . . . end:* ed. (Sir . . . morn, / Lets . . . end: Q)

59–60 ed. (*as one line* Q)

61 *immediately* i.e. irremediably, without any possible intervention of grace (OED 1)

64 *Custom* Common use

65–8 ed. (O . . . life? / What . . . Man: / Would . . . bed: Q)

71 *undoubted issues* i.e. indubitably legitimate offspring

72 *sober* modest

74–5 *things . . . Nile* i.e. crocodiles (Marston used a similar image a year later in *Sophonisba*, Syphax speaking of Zanthia at the end of III.i: 'I'll use this Zanthia, / And trust her as our dogs drink dangerous Nile, / Only for thirst, then fly the crocodile.')

Whose use makes weak, whose company doth shame,
Whose bed doth beggar, issue doth defame!

Enter FRANCESCHINA

FRANCESCHINA

Mettre Freevill live! Ha, ha! Live at Mestre Shatewe's! Mush at Mettre Shatewe's! Freevill is dead; Malheureux sall hang; and, sweet divil! dat Beatrice would but run mad, dat she would but run mad, den me would dance and sing. [*to Freevill*] Mettre Don Dubon, me pray ye now go to Mestress Beatrice; tell her Freevill is sure dead, and dat he curse herself especially, for dat he was sticked in her quarrel, swearing in his last gasp dat if it had bin in mine quarrels 'twould never have grieved him.

FREEVILL

I will.

FRANCESCHINA

Pridee do, and say anyting dat vill vex her.

FREEVILL

Let me alone to vex her.

FRANCESCHINA

Vill you? Vill you mak-a her run mad? Here, take dis ring; say me scorn to wear anyting dat was hers or his. I pridee torment her. Ick cannot love her; she honest and virtuous, forsooth!

FREEVILL

Is she so? O vile creature! Then let me alone with her.

FRANCESCHINA

Vat, vill you mak-a her mad? Seet, by min trat, be pretta servan! Bush! [*kisses him*] Ick sall go to bet now. [*Exit*]

FREEVILL

Mischief, whither wilt thou? O thou tearless woman!

80–8 ed. (*as irregular verse* Q)
81 *Mush at* i.e. much may he be (I bet he isn't)
84 *Dubon* i.e. Fr. *du bon* (= of the good), pointing to Freevill's obscured but morally honourable role here. We may remember that the disguised Freevill is introduced as 'a stranger' at IV.iii.36.
92–5 ed. (*as irregular verse* Q)
93 *say* ed. (sea Q)
96 *let ... her* This now means more than the 'trust me' of 91, i.e. that she will soon cease being honest and virtuous if left alone with me for while.
97–8 ed. (Vat ... trat, / Be ... now. Q)
be ... servan i.e. you are a pretty servant
98 *Bush* Buss, kiss
s.d. *kisses him* (*not in* Q)

How monstrous is thy devil! the end of hell as thee!
How miserable were it to be virtuous,
If thou couldst prosper!
I'll to my love, the faithful Beatrice;
She has wept enough, and, faith, dear soul, too much.
But yet how sweet it is to think how dear
One's life was to his love, how mourned his death!
'Tis joy not to be expressed with breath.
But, O, let him that would such passion drink
Be quiet of his speech, and only think. *Exit*

[Act V, Scene ii]

Enter BEATRICE *and* CRISPINELLA

BEATRICE

Sister, cannot a woman kill herself? Is it not lawful to die when we should not live?

CRISPINELLA

O sister, 'tis a question not for us; we must do what God will.

BEATRICE

What God will? Alas, can torment be his glory? or our grief his pleasure? Does not the nurse's nipple, juiced over with wormwood, bid the child it should not suck? And does not heaven, when it hath made our breath bitter unto us, say we should not live? O my best sister,
To suffer wounds when one may 'scape this rod
Is against nature, that is, against God.

CRISPINELLA

Good sister, do not make me weep. Sure Freevill was not false:
I'll gage my life that strumpet, out of craft,
And some close second end, hath maliced him.

BEATRICE

O sister, if he were not false, whom have I lost!
If he were, what grief to such unkindness!
From head to foot I am all misery;

100 *as* is as
100–2 ed. (How . . . Deuill, / The . . . thee. / How . . . prosper? Q)
105–6 ed. (But . . . thinke / How . . . death. Q)

10–11 ed. (*as prose* Q)
14 ed. (*as prose* Q)
15 *maliced* maligned
17 *to* would be appropriate response to; or perhaps, could be compared to

Only in this, some justice I have found:
My grief is like my love, beyond all bound.

Enter NURSE [PUTIFER]

[PUTIFER]
My servant, Master Caqueteur, desires to visit you.

CRISPINELLA
For grief's sake, keep him out! His discourse is like the long word *Honorificabilitudinitatibus*, a great deal of sound and no sense. His company is like a parenthesis to a discourse: you may admit it, or leave it out, it makes no matter.

Enter FREEVILL *in his* [*disguise*]

FREEVILL
By your leave, sweet creatures.

CRISPINELLA
Sir, all I can yet say of you is you are uncivil.

FREEVILL
You must deny it. [*to Beatrice*] By your sorrow's leave,
I bring some music to make sweet your grief.

BEATRICE
Whate'er you please. O, break, my heart!
Canst thou yet pant? O, dost thou yet survive?
Thou didst not love him if thou now canst live!

FREEVILL (*sings*)
O Love, how strangely sweet
Are thy weak passions,
That love and joy should meet
In selfsame fashions!
O, who can tell
The cause why this should move?
But only this,
No reason ask of love!

[*Beatrice*] *swoons*

19 *justice* i.e. equal dealing

21 s.p. ed. (*Nurse.* Q)

23 *Honorificabilitudinitatibus* A grandiose extension of the Latin word for honourableness, put in the dative/ablative plural to make it longer

26 s.d. *disguise* 1633 (*discourse* Q)

34 s.d. ed. (*this and s.d. at 41 included in* Q*'s single s.d. at this point, 'He sings, she sounds.'*)

34–41 The song is not recorded elsewhere.

35 *weak* causing weakness

CRISPINELLA
Hold, peace! The gentlest soul is swooned. – O my best sister!

FREEVILL
Ha! get you gone, close the doors. [*to Nurse Putifer*] – My Beatrice!

[*Exit* NURSE PUTIFER; FREEVILL] *discovers himself*

Cursed be my indiscreet trials! O my immeasurably loving!

CRISPINELLA
She stirs; give air, she breathes!

BEATRICE
Where am I, ha? How have I slipped off life?
Am I in heaven? O my lord, though not loving,
By our eternal being, yet give me leave
To rest by thy dear side. Am I not in heaven?

FREEVILL
O eternally much loved, recollect your spirits!

BEATRICE
Ha, you do speak! I do see you; I do live!
I would not die now. Let me not burst with wonder!

FREEVILL
Call up your blood; I live to honour you
As the admired glory of your sex.
Nor ever hath my love been false to you;
Only I presumed to try your faith too much,
For which I most am grieved.

CRISPINELLA
Brother, I must be plain with you; you have wronged us.

[FREEVILL]
I am not so covetous to deny it;
But yet, when my discourse hath stayed your quaking,
You will be smoother-lipped; and the delight
And satisfaction which we all have got
Under these strange disguisings, when you know,
You will be mild and quiet, forget at last.
It is much joy to think on sorrows past.

44 s.d. (*not in* Q)
45 s.d. *Exit NURSE PUTIFER*; (*not in* Q); *discovers himself* removes his disguise
46 *trials* testing of you
52 *loved* 1633 (laued Q)
61 s.p. 1633 (*not in* Q)
61 *covetous* eager
63 *smoother-lipped* less harsh in speech

BEATRICE

Do you, then, live? And are you not untrue?
Let me not die with joy! Pleasure's more extreme
Than grief; there's nothing sweet to man but mean.

FREEVILL

Heaven cannot be too gracious to such goodness.
I shall discourse to you the several chances;
But hark, I must yet rest disguised. [*reassumes disguise*]
The sudden close of many drifts now meet;
Where pleasure hath some profit, art is sweet.

Enter TYSEFEW

TYSEFEW

News, news, news, news!

CRISPINELLA

Oysters, oysters, oysters, oysters!

TYSEFEW

Why, is not this well now? Is not this better than louring and pouting and puling, which is hateful to the living and vain to the dead? Come, come, you must live by the quick, when all is done. And for my own part, let my wife laugh at me when I am dead, so she'll smile upon me whilst I live. But to see a woman whine, and yet keep her eyes dry; mourn, and yet keep her cheeks fat; nay, to see a woman claw her husband by the feet when he is dead, that would have scratched him by the face when he was living – this now is somewhat ridiculous.

70 *there's ... mean* This is a reference to the Aristotelian 'golden mean', that nothing should be experienced to excess.

71–4 ed. (*as prose* Q)

72 *several chances* events as they fell out

74 *drifts* plots, intrigues

77 'Crispinella mockingly treats Tysefew's interruption as though it were a London street cry' (Jackson and Neill).

78–87 'I can never forget this good saying, *Jactantius maerent, quae minus dolent, They keepe a howling with most ostentation, who are lesse sorrowfull at heart* [Tacitus, *Annales* II.77]. Their lowring and puling is hatefull to the living, and vaine to the dead. *Wee shall easily dispence with them to laugh at us when we are dead, upon condition they smile upon us while wee live.* Is not this the way to revive a man with spite; that he who hath spitten in my face when I was living, shal come and claw my feet when I am dead? If there be any honour for a woman to weepe for hir husband, it belongs to hir that hath smiled upon him when she had him. Such as have wept when they lived, let them laugh when they are dead, as well outwardly as inwardly' (Montaigne II.xxxv.594–5).

79 *puling* whining

80 *quick* living

CRISPINELLA
Lord, how you prate!

TYSEFEW
And yet I was afraid, i'faith, that I should ha' seen a garland on this beauty's hearse; but time, truth, experience, and variety are great doers with women.

CRISPINELLA
But what's the news? The news, I pray you.

TYSEFEW
I pray you! Ne'er pray me, for by your leave you may command me. This 'tis:
The public sessions, which this day is past,
Hath doomed to death ill-fortuned Malheureux.

CRISPINELLA
But, sir, we heard he offered to make good
That Freevill lived at Shatewe's the jeweller's –

BEATRICE
And that 'twas but a plot betwixt them two.

TYSEFEW
O, ay, ay, he gaged his life with it; but know,
When all approached the test, Shatewe denied
He saw or heard of any such complot,
Or of Freevill; so that his own defence
Appeared so false that, like a madman's sword,
He struck his own heart. He hath the course of law
And instantly must suffer. But the jest
(If hanging be a jest, as many make it)
Is to take notice of one Mulligrub,
A sharking vintner.

FREEVILL
What of him, sir?

TYSEFEW
Nothing but hanging. The whoreson slave is mad before he hath lost his senses.

FREEVILL
Was his fact clear and made apparent, sir?

95–6 ed. (*as prose* Q)
97 *make good* demonstrate, prove
101 *Shatewe* 1633 (Shatews Q)
102 *complot* plot, conspiracy
108–9 ed. (*as one line* Q)
111–12 *mad . . . senses* i.e. has lost his senses in unreason before he has lost them by death
113 *fact* criminal deed

TYSEFEW
No, faith, suspicions – for 'twas thus protested:
A cloak was stolen; that cloak he had; he had it,
Himself confessed, by force. The rest of his defence
The choler of a justice wronged in wine –
Joined with malignance of some hasty jurors,
Whose wit was lighted by the justice' nose,
The knave was cast.
But, Lord, to hear his moan, his prayers, his wishes,
His zeal ill-timed, and his words unpitied,
Would make a dead man rise and smile,
Whilst he observed how fear can make men vile.

CRISPINELLA
Shall we go meet the execution?

BEATRICE
I shall be ruled by you.

TYSEFEW
By my troth, a rare motion. You must haste,
For malefactors goes like the world, upon wheels.

BEATRICE
Will you man us? [*to Freevill*] You shall be our guide.

FREEVILL
I am your servant.

TYSEFEW
Ha, servant! Zounds, I am no companion for panders!
You're best make him your love.

BEATRICE
So will I, sir; we must live by the quick, you say.

117 i.e. the choler of a drunken justice gave ill consideration to

119 i.e. the angry, drunken red nose of the judge led the jury's understanding of the matter in the direction the judge wanted

119–20 ed. (*as one line* Q)

120 *cast* cast away, condemned

127 *motion* proposal (and see pun at III.i.128n)

128 Just as the world goes rapidly on its heedless way ('upon wheels'), so all too quickly the condemned man goes in his wheeled cart to execution.

129 *man* squire (Freevill, as Dubon, was good enough to squire Franceschina at IV.iii.39, but not here for real ladies). Franceschina was setting out upon her revenge, Beatrice here to divert herself with an execution. She will know that, because Freevill lives, Malheureux will not hang, but there is always Mulligrub.

129 s.d. ed. (*printed as part of the text, after* guide *in* Q)

130 *servant* i.e. I will do as you ask; but through his disguise Freevill speaks the word in the sense of 'lover' to Beatrice, and Tysefew picks up what he thinks a grotesquely unintended sense of the word for a pander to a lady

132 *You're best* i.e. (jokingly) you'd do well to

TYSEFEW
'Sdeath o' virtue! What a damned thing's this!
Who'll trust fair faces, tears, and vows? 'Sdeath, not I!
She is a woman – that is, she can lie.

CRISPINELLA
Come, come, turn not a man of time, to make all ill
Whose goodness you conceive not, since the worst of chance
Is to crave grace for heedless ignorance.

Exeunt

[Act V, Scene iii]

Enter COCLEDEMOY *like a Sergeant*

COCLEDEMOY
So, I ha' lost my sergeant in an ecliptic mist. Drunk, horrible drunk! He is fine! So now will I fit myself; I hope this habit will do me no harm. I am an honest man already. Fit, fit, fit as a punk's tail, that serves everybody. By this time my vintner thinks of nothing but hell and sulphur; he farts fire and brimstone already. Hang toasts! the execution approacheth.

Enter SIR LIONEL, SIR HUBERT, MALHEUREUX *pinioned,* TYSEFEW, BEATRICE, FREEVILL [*disguised*], CRISPINELLA, FRANCESCHINA, *and* [*Officers with*] *halberds*

MALHEUREUX
I do not blush, although condemned by laws.
No kind of death is shameful but the cause,
Which I do know is none; and yet my lust
Hath made the one (although not cause) most just.

137 *of time* i.e. of conventional, superficial judgement
138 *conceive not* do not understand

1 *ecliptic mist* an all-eclipsing haze of alcohol
2 *fine* In view of what immediately follows, one might consider an emendation to 'fitted' (= well seen to).
fit myself see to myself (i.e. wear his uniform)
3 *do . . . harm* i.e. as the sergeant inside it would have done
honest man already i.e. now I have got this respectable uniform on
4 *punk's . . . everybody* See IV.iii.6n.
7 s.d.2 *disguised* (*not in* Q)
9 *but the cause* i.e. it is the reason for death and not the manner of it that counts (and here there is no reason for it in reality)

May I not be reprieved? Freevill is but mislodged;
Some lethargy hath seized him – no, much malice.
Do not lay blood upon your souls with good intents;
Men may do ill, and law sometime repents.

COCLEDEMOY *picks* MALHEUREUX'*pocket of his purse*

SIR LIONEL
Sir, sir, prepare; vain is all lewd defence.

MALHEUREUX
Conscience was law, but now law's conscience.
My endless peace is made, and to the poor –
My purse, my purse!

COCLEDEMOY
Ay, sir, and it shall please you, the poor has your purse already.

MALHEUREUX
You are a wily man.
[*to Franceschina*] But now, thou source of devils, O, how I loathe
The very memory of that I adored!
He that's of fair blood, well-miened, of good breeding,
Best famed, of sweet acquaintance and true friends,
And would with desperate impudence lose all these,
And hazard landing at this fatal shore,
Let him ne'er kill nor steal, but love a whore!

FRANCESCHINA
De man does rave. Tink o' Got, tink o' Got! and bid de flesh, de world, and the dible farewell.

MALHEUREUX
Farewell!

12 *mislodged* lodged in the wrong place

16 *lewd* poor, ill-conceived, worthless

18 *endless* eternal

to the poor The condemned man, if he had money, generally gave an alms to the poor if he was playing his part rightly.

22 *wily man* ed. (Welyman Q). Perhaps we could read 'Welshman' (in the sense = thief), especially in view of Cocledemoy's affected Welshness (in the manner of Evans in *The Merry Wives of Windsor*) as the play ends: his 'prittles and prattles', 'bibbles and babbles' (88–9); his 'metheglins' (106); his distinctively Welsh plurals (91–2, 123). It seems appropriate that the Welsh should come in for their share of satire from a man who has already, as the barber, impersonated a Scotsman (II.iii.15n).

27 *impudence* boldness, effrontery

FREEVILL
Farewell. FREEVILL *discovers himself*
FRANCESCHINA
Vat is't you say? Ha!
FREEVILL
Sir, your pardon; with my this defence,
Do not forget protested violence
Of your low affections; no requests,
No arguments of reason, no known danger,
No assured wicked bloodiness,
Could draw your heart from this damnation.
MALHEUREUX
Why, stay!
FRANCESCHINA
Unprosperous divel! vat sall me do now?
FREEVILL
Therefore, to force you from the truer danger,
I wrought the feigned, suffering this fair devil
In shape of woman to make good her plot;
And, knowing that the hook was deeply fast,
I gave her line at will, till with her own vain strivings
See here she's tired. O thou comely damnation!
Dost think that vice is not to be withstood?
O, what is woman merely made of blood!
SIR LIONEL
You 'maze us all; let us not be lost in darkness.
FREEVILL
All shall be lighted, but this time and place
Forbids longer speech; only what you can think
Has been extremely ill is only hers.

33 *Farewell* In the sense here 'fare well, may things go well with you' and not like Malheureux' 'goodbye'
33 s.d. ed. (*after 32* Q)
34 *say* ed. (sea Q)
35 *my this* this my
39 *wicked bloodiness* i.e. of Franceschina's intent
40 *damnation* i.e. Franceschina
42 *Unprosperous divel* Franceschina refers to herself and the failure of her plans for revenge.
45 *shape* ed. (shaps Q)
make good carry through
48 *tired* pulled in, exhausted, like a caught fish
50 *blood* violent passion
51 *in darkness* i.e. as to the shape of the intrigue

SIR LIONEL

To severest prison with her! –
With what heart canst live? what eyes behold a face?

FRANCESCHINA

Ick vill not speak. Torture, torture your fill,
For me am worse than hanged; me ha' lost my will.

Exit FRANCESCHINA *with the guard*

SIR LIONEL

To the extremest whip and jail!

FREEVILL

Frolic, how is it, sir?

MALHEUREUX

I am myself. How long was't ere I could
Persuade my passion to grow calm to you!
Rich sense makes good bad language, and a friend
Should weigh no action, but the action's end.
I am now worthy yours, when, before,
The beast of man, loose blood, distempered us.
He that lust rules cannot be virtuous.

Enter MULLIGRUB, MISTRESS MULLIGRUB, *and Officers*

OFFICER

On afore there! Room for the prisoner!

MULLIGRUB

I pray you, do not lead me to execution through Cheapside. I owe Master Burnish, the goldsmith, money, and I fear he'll set a sergeant on my back for it.

COCLEDEMOY

Trouble not your sconce, my Christian brother, but have an eye unto the main chance. I will warrant your shoulders; as for your neck, Plinius Secundus, or Marcus Tullius Cicero, or somebody it is, says that a threefold cord is hardly broken.

55–6 ed. (To . . . liue? / What . . . face? Q)

60 *sir* ed. (Sirs Q)

63 *bad language* i.e. the 'bad language' of Freevill's deceit of Malheureux

66 *distempered us* distorted our friendship

68 *prisoner* (prisoners Q)

69–71 'One who was led to the gallowes, desired it might not be thorow such a street, for feare a Merchant should set a Serjant on his backe, for an old debt' (Montaigne I.xl.323).

72 *sconce* joking term for the 'head'
brother ed. (Brothers Q)

73 *main chance* i.e. it is your neck you should be worrying about

75–6 *a . . . broken* 'a threefold cord is not quickly broken' (Ecclesiastes 4.12)

MULLIGRUB

Well, I am not the first honest man that hath been cast away, and I hope shall not be the last.

COCLEDEMOY

O, sir, have a good stomach and maws; you shall have a joyful supper.

MULLIGRUB

In troth, I have no stomach to it. And it please you, take my trencher; I use to fast at nights.

MISTRESS MULLIGRUB

O husband, I little thought you should have come to think on God thus soon! Nay, and you had been hanged deservedly, it would never have grieved me. I have known of many honest, innocent men have been hanged deservedly – but to be cast away for nothing!

COCLEDEMOY

Good woman, hold your peace, your prittles and your prattles, your bibbles and your babbles; for I pray you hear me in private. I am a widower, and you are almost a widow; shall I be welcome to your houses, to your tables, and your other things?

MISTRESS MULLIGRUB

I have a piece of mutton and a featherbed for you at all times. [*to Mulligrub*] I pray, make haste.

MULLIGRUB

I do here make my confession. If I owe any man anything, I do heartily forgive him; if any man owe me anything, let him pay my wife.

78 *I hope* This, as it were, interpolation into a usual sentiment is typical of Mulligrub.

79–82 'Another answered his confessor, who promised him he should sup that night with our Saviour in heaven, Goe thither your selfe to supper, for I use to fast a nights' (Montaigne I.xl.323).

79 *maws* throat, gullet

82 *trencher* platter (for food)

83–4 *O . . . soon* The echo of Evan's reproof to Mistress Quickly in *The Merry Wives of Windsor* IV.i, which we have in the following speech (see V.iii.22n), clearly brings with it here Mistress Quickly's account of the death of Falstaff in *Henry V* II.iii.

84–7 *Nay . . . nothing* '*Socrates* his wife, exasperated her griefe by this circumstance; *Good Lord* (said she) *how unjustly doe these bad judges put him to death!* What? *Wouldest thou rather they should execute me justly?* replide he to her' (Montaigne II.xii.370).

88–9 *prittles . . . babbles* worthless chatter

93 *piece of mutton* With a sexual innuendo deriving from the idea of flesh (see III.iii.23–4n).

COCLEDEMOY

I will look to your wife's payment, I warrant you.

MULLIGRUB

And now, good yoke-fellow, leave thy poor Mulligrub.

MISTRESS MULLIGRUB

Nay, then I were unkind; i'faith, I will not leave you until I have seen you hang.

COCLEDEMOY

But brother, brother, you must think of your sins and iniquities. You have been a broacher of profane vessels; you have made us drink of the juice of the whore of Babylon. For whereas good ale, perries, braggets, ciders, and metheglins was the true ancient British and Troyan drinks, you ha' brought in Popish wines, Spanish wines, French wines, *tam Marti quam Mercurio*, both muscadine and malmsey, to the subversion, staggering, and sometimes overthrow of many a good Christian. You ha' been a great jumbler. O, remember the sins of your nights! for your night works ha' been unsavoury in the taste of your customers.

MULLIGRUB

I confess, I confess, and I forgive as I would be forgiven! Do you know one Cocledemoy?

COCLEDEMOY

O, very well. Know him! An honest man he is, and a comely, an upright dealer with his neighbours, and their wives speak good things of him.

100 *I . . . unkind* i.e. I would be behaving unnaturally, not as befits a wife

102 *brother, brother* ed. (brothers, brothers Q)

103 *profane vessels* wine-casks; women's bodies (in the Puritan cant of the whole of this speech)

104 *whore of Babylon* i.e. the Catholic church

105 *perries* a kind of cider made from pears
braggets honey and ale fermented together
ciders ed. (*Syders* Q)

106 *metheglins* 'spiced or medicated variety of mead, originally peculiar to Wales' (OED)
Troyan Refers to the mediaeval legend that Brutus, the great grandson of the Trojan hero, Aeneas, settled the island of Britain, with London as a new Troy.

108 *tam . . . Mercurio* 'as much for Mars as for Mercury', i.e. as drinks breeding both valour (Mars) and wit (Mercury)

108–9 *both . . . malmsey* A mock translation of the previous Latin phrase, using the names of two sweet, fortified wines from France and Spain

111 *jumbler* See III.ii.38–9 & n; 'jumble' is also slang for 'copulate', and both the adulterating of wine and illicit sex take place at night.

117 *upright* With a sexual innuendo of 'erect'

118 *wives . . . him* i.e. in his 'erect' dealings with them

MULLIGRUB

Well, whereso'er he is, or whatsoe'er he is, I'll take it on my death he's the cause of my hanging. I heartily forgive him; and if he would come forth he might save me, for he only knows the why and the wherefore.

COCLEDEMOY

You do, from your hearts and midriffs and entrails, forgive him, then? You will not let him rot in rusty irons, procure him to be hanged in lousy linen without a song, and, after he is dead, piss on his grave?

MULLIGRUB

That hard heart of mine has procured all this, but I forgive as I would be forgiven.

COCLEDEMOY

Hang toasts, my worshipful Mulligrub! Behold thy Cocledemoy, my fine vintner, my castrophomical fine boy! behold and see! [*discovers himself*]

TYSEFEW

Bliss o' the blessed, who would but look for two knaves here!

COCLEDEMOY

No knave, worshipful friend, no knave; for, observe, honest Cocledemoy restores whatsoever he has got, to make you know that whatsoe'er he has done has been only *euphoniae gratia* – for wit's sake. I acquit this vintner as he has acquitted me. All has been done for emphasis of wit, my fine boy, my worshipful friends.

TYSEFEW

Go, you are a flattering knave.

COCLEDEMOY

I am so; 'tis a good thriving trade. It comes forward better than the seven liberal sciences or the nine cardinal virtues,

125 *song* i.e. psalm (see III.ii.11)

130 *castrophomical* See II.i.194n.

135 *Cocledemoy . . . got* It would be an effective theatrical touch if Cocledemoy gave back the goblet here, and would further motivate Mulligrub's line at 147.

136–7 *euphoniae gratia* i.e. for the sake of euphony, pleasant sound, here translated as 'wit' by Cocledemoy because the elements of the witty intrigue of the play do indeed here make a pleasing concord

141 *comes forward* flourishes

142 *seven . . . sciences* The seven subjects of the mediaeval university curriculum, designed to produce a free (liberal) man: the *trivium* consisted of grammar, logic and rhetoric; the *quadrivium* of arithmetic, geometry, music and astronomy.
nine . . . virtues They are usually seven: faith, hope, charity, justice, prudence, temperence, fortitude; presumably Cocledemoy emphasises his sense of their importance by making them nine (like the nine Muses).

which may well appear in this: you shall never have flattering knave turn courtier, and yet I have read of many courtiers that have turned flattering knaves.

SIR HUBERT
Was't even but so? Why, then, all's well!

MULLIGRUB
I could even weep for joy!

MISTRESS MULLIGRUB
I could weep, too, but God knows for what!

TYSEFEW
Here's another tack to be given – your son and daughter.

SIR HUBERT
Is't possible? Heart, ay, all my heart! Will you be joined here?

TYSEFEW
Yes, faith, father; marriage and hanging are spun both in one hour.

COCLEDEMOY
Why, then, my worshipful good friends, I bid myself most heartily welcome to your merry nuptials and wanton jigga-joggies.

[*Coming forward and addressing the audience*]

And now, my very fine Heliconian gallants, and you, my worshipful friends in the middle region:
If with content our hurtless mirth hath been,
Let your pleased minds at our much care be seen;
For he shall find, that slights such trivial wit,
'Tis easier to reprove than better it.
We scorn to fear, and yet we fear to swell;
We do not hope 'tis best: 'tis all, if well.

Exeunt

149 *tack* addition, joining
157 *Heliconian* i.e. devoted to the Muses, who dwelt on Mount Helicon
158 *middle region* i.e. a little below the 'gallants' in social standing, and in a different part of the auditorium
160 *at . . . seen* ed. (as our much care hath bin Q)
163 *swell* i.e. in pride at a good play